Weaving a Fabric of Unity

Conversations on Education and Development

Haleh Arbab
Gustavo Correa
Bradley Wilson

CRED
CENTER FOR RESEARCH
IN EDUCATION
FOR DEVELOPMENT, INC

Library of Congress Control Number: 2025930877

Center for Research in Education for Development, Inc.
7369 Westport Place
West Palm Beach, Florida 33413
U.S.A.
info@researchfordevelopment.org
www.researchfordevelopment.org

Cover art: Sky Glabush, *Flare and Glide Off*, 2023
Cover design by Ezra Hopkins

Distributed by West Virginia University Press for CRED. For EU safety/GPSR
concerns, please direct inquiries to WVUPress@mail.wvu.edu or our physical
mailing address at West Virginia University Press / PO Box 6295 / West Virginia
University / Morgantown, WV, 26508, USA.

...once again she shuddered with the evidence that time was not passing, as she had just admitted, but that it was turning in a circle.

Gabriel García Márquez, *One Hundred Years of Solitude*

Dedication

This book is dedicated to all the souls who embraced the vision kindled half a century ago by the initiators of FUNDAEC and who have labored throughout the years to transform this dream into reality. Their unwavering commitment and steadfast service have laid the bedrock upon which the institution's triumphs stand tall. Though some are mentioned within these pages, countless others—whose faith, effort, and dedication were equally vital—remain unnamed. Without their devotion to the cause of development, the story woven in this book could never have been told.

Table of Contents

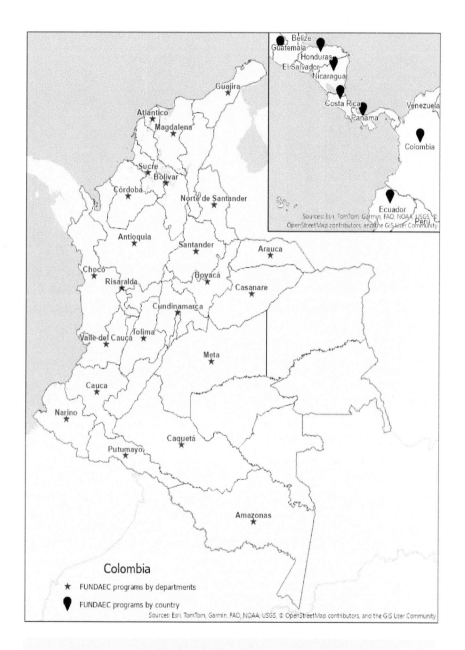

Location of FUNDAEC programs in Latin America

Preface

By Bradley Wilson

...the victims of these erroneous policies are not only the broken families living partly in the village and partly in the slums of the city. The entire planet has suffered from its infatuation with a certain brand of industrialization and urbanization, as its leaders and policymakers, following their dreams and living in islands of prosperity, have lost touch both with the soul of the masses and with nature.

Farzam Arbab, *The Lab, the Temple, and the Market*[1]

I f we look back at the human drama lived by the first generations of the 21st century, we must ask ourselves: What lessons did we learn from the last generations of the 20th century? What wisdom can our parents and grandparents offer us? What kind of insight might we draw from a close inspection of the lived experiences of these three successive generations in the life of humanity?[2] Students of history, geography, and development would tell you that the generations coinciding with 1974–2024 have navigated one of the most distressing periods in human history. They have lived through one of the most intense phases of urbanization, industrialization, globalization, and other forces that have imposed new patterns of life—both sociological and ecological—the world over.

Reconsidering our path from the 1970s to the present is an exercise that is not for the faint of heart. Emboldened by both geopolitical control and technological advances resulting from major investments in a global military conflict that threatened to annihilate humanity by the end of

---

[1] Arbab, F. (2000) 'Promoting a discourse on science, religion, and development' in Harper, S. (ed.) *The lab, the temple, and the market: Reflections at the intersection of science, religion, and development.* Canada: IDRC; Europe and the United States: Kumarian Press.

[2] The average period of a generation is considered to be about 25 years during which time children are born and grow up, become adults, and begin to have children.

1945,[3] by 1970, a growing belief in the primacy of modern science and the superiority of modernizing development strategies was taking root in the long shadow of colonialism. Many young people who had been mobilized into social movements aspiring to fulfill the promise of global peace and an era of shared prosperity saw the retreat of formal colonialism, the advance of civil rights and gender equality, the rise of environmental consciousness, and the push for human rights in various countries. However, by the 1970s, they faced a harsh and disorienting reality that many of the gains they had achieved in the 1960s were disappearing under the pressure of, and demand for, a new global economic order. The political and economic reality they had struggled to change was still quite out of their reach.

Seen from the vantage point of today in 2024, the double exposure of social and ecological disintegration caused by the expansion of this global economic order created a level of human vulnerability unseen in previous centuries. The Green Revolution's devastating impact on food systems and rural life, the insatiable thirst for the world's resources, and the unquenchable demand for the world's labor to produce commodities for an age of high consumption have created tremendous interdependencies; unimaginable disparities in wealth; displaced billions of people from their ancestral homelands; and reconfigured daily life in every region of the globe. Even the most ardent proponents of this global economic vision would agree that this order was not requested; it was not the dream of the post-war generation, but rather, it was unconditionally thrust upon peoples and ecologies across the planet.[4] The new order fundamentally transformed climate, forests, rivers, soils, agricultural practices and food systems, working lives, cultures and traditions, homeplaces, and families. No one left the end of the 20th century unscathed.

> The all-pervading disease of the modern world is the total imbalance between city and countryside, an imbalance in terms of wealth, power, culture, attraction and hope. The former has become over-extended and the latter has atrophied. The city has become the universal magnet, while rural life has lost its savour... The prevailing lack of balance, based on the age-old exploitation of

---

[3] In the preparations for the Trinity Test, the first to unleash the power of atomic weaponry, Robert Oppenheimer feared that nuclear bombs may in fact set the atmosphere on fire and end the world. He is quoted in 1965 as saying: "We knew the world would not be the same. A few people laughed; a few people cried. Most people were silent. I remembered the line from the Hindu scripture, the *Bhagavad Gita*; Vishnu is trying to persuade the prince that he should do his duty, and to impress him, takes on his multi-armed form and says, 'Now I am become Death, the destroyer of worlds.' I suppose we [the scientists who enabled the atomic bomb] all thought that, one way or another."

[4] Many who are proponents of the present global economic order argued that it must be imposed, often through policy measures required by states, international banks, and other development agencies. In the words of some proponents, shifting the existing order required "shock therapy" to break the traditional community psychology of the previous generation to impress upon them the rules and habits of the economic growth model.

countryman and raw material producer, today threatens all countries throughout the world, the rich even more than the poor. To restore a proper balance between city and rural life is perhaps the greatest task in front of modern man.[5]

Central to establishing the global economic order was a rather stark geographical reality: the exploitation, destruction, and abandonment of the countryside, its peoples, and resources. As E.F. Schumacher eloquently explained on the cusp of 1974, the imbalance between city and countryside "threatens all countries throughout the world."[6] In the early 1970s, this observation might have seemed a bit far-fetched. In 1970, the global urban population was just 1.3 billion. However, by 2020, the urban population was 4.4 billion. When the pandemic struck in 2020, more people lived in cities than had previously existed on planet Earth just 50 years before.

The speculations that urbanization and globalization would improve the conditions of rural and urban society have not generated uniform results. The promise of a better modern life in the cities has not materialized for the majority of their inhabitants across the world. The demands of the city place great pressure on the people and resources of the countryside as well. Yet, the vulnerabilities created by urbanization do not reveal themselves to everyone in the same way. Across a highly segregated world, there are those living in "islands of prosperity" while others live in a sea of uncertainty and misery. For some, the pandemic was the great revealer of these realities. The shutdowns and lock-ins that short-circuited the global food system created a period in which segregated neighborhoods, rich and poor, suddenly experienced the same uncertainties and fear to which the poor's children are daily accustomed.

When economic activities ground to a halt in a matter of weeks, it demonstrated to all the great degree of these human vulnerabilities, just under the veil of normalcy, caused by thrusting billions of people from the countryside into the cities during the past 50 years. Looking back at the quiet streets across New York, Bogota, Nairobi, Delhi, and Beijing—as people locked in their quarters questioned how many days they had left before food rations ran out—Schumacher's prophetic words have a different resonance. The pandemic made clear—to those who had forgotten or had never experienced poverty—the insecurity of this order for those who rely upon a steady income, decent work, and global supply chains to put food on the table. The source of the problem—what Schumacher called a "disease of the modern world"—was not the coronavirus. The virus merely unveiled the preexisting conditions.

---

[5] Schumacher, E. F. (1973/2011) *Small is beautiful: A study of economics as if people mattered*. New York: Random House.

[6] Ibid.

The forces at work that led to rural and urban change from 1974 to 2024 were like an uncontrolled wildfire tearing through a forest, burning down many of the foundations of traditional rural community life remaining—even after colonialism and the ruinous wars of the 20th century—pressing billions of people, the children of two generations, to search for their livelihoods elsewhere. Thrust out of the burning forest of past conventions and traditions, rural humanity became an increasingly urban humanity. In doing so, rural humanity lost its ancestral land and territorial ties to the natural world and was rendered ever more vulnerable to the changes and chances of a world governed by the new global economic order. The result for them was a frenetic dependence on, or forced resignation to use, the very tools and models that had set the world ablaze in the first place. Within just a few short decades after the 1970s, even the most ardent supporters of the economic growth models proposed could not escape the fire that, as Bob Marley so prophetically remarked, "was burning down everything."[7]

By the 1980s, less than two decades into the grand experiment, many in the global community realized that the social, environmental, and even economic consequences and costs of the actions taken to advance unbridled economic growth were unsustainable. An emerging discourse pressing for greater attention to the negative social and ecological effects of economic growth—sustainable development—emerged on the scene quietly in 1983 and gained global notoriety by 1992 at the United Nations (UN) Earth Summit, the first of its kind and a precursor to the climate change conferences that would follow annually in future decades. Yet, though there was growing consensus among physical and social scientists that an imbalance of people and the planet was well underway, political will continued to favor preserving business as usual.

Currently, more than 30 years since the UN Earth Summit in 1992 and 40 years since the Brundtland Commission first articulated the concept of sustainable development, the global economic order to which we are tied and the goals of economic growth remain largely intact and seem to be accelerating. It is understandable, then, for a generation born after 2000 to have become impatient, having witnessed the suffering of their parents and grandparents. And some have become cynical about the future. The scientific understanding of the problem, the economic pain experienced by communities, and the consensus that something must be done to reconnect city and country and make the world whole again are as old as, or older than, their parents and grandparents. This, then, raises the question for the youth of today: Do the past generations

---

[7] "Because now the fire is out of control, panic in the city, wicked weeping for their gold! Everywhere this fire is burning, destroying and melting their gold, destroying and wasting their souls." - Bob Marley, *Ride Natty Ride, Survival* (1979)

think the world can change for the better, or have they grown too cynical as well?

The Breach

For people who lived the full arc of this story, those born well before the 1970s, what you have just read may resonate with the experience of your generation. You may perceive it acutely, with a sensibility that the current generation cannot begin to fathom. The revelations and disappointments, hopes and setbacks are difficult to relive. For those born more recently, the younger generations of today raised since 2000, you might read this and ask yourselves, how could you all let this happen? Why didn't you put out the fire? How could our futures be mortgaged and our generation be burdened by these mistakes? And for those of us born in the middle, between the generations who lived the arc of this period but know nothing of before, and see the challenges of the future for our children, we witness a widening breach between and among those who have lived this history together—a breach that must be overcome.

No matter which generation you are from, the sense of danger, disorientation, and despair lurking around the corner has led many of our friends, family, coworkers, and collaborators into an unfortunate cul-de-sac and a cynical sense of reality: a disbelief in the possibility that things could change for the better. What is of concern is not only the loss of hope but the growing divide or breach—la brecha—in the generations. The breach has ripped apart a fabric of intergenerational understanding—a social fabric necessary for building a better future for humanity—a fabric woven through generational dialogue, mutual learning, and knowledge-sharing foundational to the human spirit, development, and civilization.

"Why is hope in such short supply?" one might ask. As a college professor at a public university in a poor Appalachian state struggling with the issues described above, I witness firsthand, every semester, another group of students who are wishing for a way to—as Walter Benjamin wrote of the angel of history in 1940—"awaken the dead" and "make whole what has been smashed."[8] It is so clear in their eyes, words, and actions that they genuinely and earnestly want to make a meaningful contribution to the rehabilitation of the fortunes of humanity. But, as I have witnessed, their wings are caught in the winds of circumstances far out of their control. Pressed into difficult financial situations and subject to unrelenting political and commercial propaganda, they become, at times, distrustful of past generations of intellectuals and

---

[8] Benjamin, W. (1940/2020) 'Theses on the philosophy of history', in Bronner, S.E. and Kellner, D. M. (eds.) *Critical theory and society: A reader.* New York: Routledge, pp. 255-263.

practitioners committed to social change. Now, looking 25 years into the future, they are setting out in search of answers to questions that, over time, have inevitably drifted away from their moorings, the reference points. Young people today—as peasants dispossessed from their land, fisherfolk pulled away from their seas, or pastoralists driven from their green pastures—are like wanderers searching for solutions to problems in uncharted territory.

While an older generation may have grown weary or might question their own wisdom, the younger generation, who have grown up entirely in a digital age, are hyper-connected to a world full of information. What they lack is not opinions, ideas, and a range of solutions to address, in varying degrees, all the world's ills, but rather unpatronizing wisdom from past generations that could help them sift through it all. The youth I work with desire knowledge and wisdom but, understandably, question its foundations given the present state of things. They want older generations to take them seriously, not patronize or sell them a false narrative. They seek trust but wonder how the past generations, on their watch, allowed the world to get this far off course. They want to know why things aren't changing. They want to know what to do.

Young people today also feel they have much to learn from the previous generations, their elders. In the 1960s and 1970s, many idealistic young people just like them, participating in movements seeking to stem the tide of the new global economic order, found great opportunity by pursuing a university education. Some would become dedicated physical and social scientists who would travel to all the corners of the world. Many would become embedded in rural and urban communities and dedicate their lives to supporting processes of social, economic, and environmental transformation. While these intrepid souls were few among their generation overall, they had an outsized impact on the course of intellectual and social history and would shape the direction of fields like development studies for decades to follow.

Through them and their studies, they created an archive of biophysical, historical, and ethnographic accounts explaining shifts in rural and urban life: they conducted nuanced analyses highlighting how the political economy of global market integration marched forward lockstep with ecological degradation. These studies were not stodgy or lacking in moral inquiry and insight. Immeasurably more detailed than any artificial intelligence, satellite image, quantitative data set, or digital map could ever replicate—these ethnographic accounts would provide a sense of the harsh realities confronted by rural peoples across the world and of the moral indignation the global economic order caused both researchers and the communities with whom they lived and studied. At times, these trained scientists drifted into the poetic, seeking artful ways to explain the contradictions of a society being bent to the will of irrational economic logic: to produce for global markets rather than sustain the families and communities within their immediate surroundings, as they had for millennia.

> Instead of man being the aim of production, production is the aim of man and wealth the aim of production; instead of tools and the productive mechanism in general liberating man from the slavery of toil, man has become the slave of tools; and the industry has become synonymous with business and people have been duped into asking, 'what's good for business?' instead of, 'what is business good for?'[9]

Rather than seeing the march of social change as some natural process or economic growth as an inevitable, rational, or desirable logic, these scientists observed the very man-made mechanisms reorienting people's thoughts, practices, and relationships toward their environments and one another. They wrote books, taught classes, built academic programs, shaped policy, and created conditions for universities to teach students about what was happening in the world and why it mattered. It was urgent, meaningful work.

One of these areas of intellectual dedication of the generations born in the past century concerned itself with peasant studies, agrarian change, human ecology, regional studies, and what would later become the field of development studies. In the transdisciplinary fields of anthropology, geography, and physical sciences—agronomy, biology, forestry, civil engineering, climatology, and hydrology—scholars trained in universities observed these changes in rural life. They recorded and sought to conceptualize the patterns of change taking place, the disequilibrium of communal life upset by what they witnessed firsthand. The field of political ecology and environmental justice research—to which I trace my intellectual awakening—began with rigorous studies conducted in rural communities undergoing violent change brought about by political and economic integration into global markets through capitalist articulation with global commodity chains and through the mounting toxicity encountered in water, fields, foods, towns, and neighborhoods.

Such scholarly work was, and is, quite unfashionable and highly disregarded by the academic establishment, let alone the arenas of policy-making. In most cases, the expectations for university-trained scientists were to "get with the program," attract research funding, and train generations to serve the rollout of the global economic order using programs intended to accelerate its reach through policy, planning, implementation, and evaluation. Yet these other scholars, unfashionable as they were, also achieved academic positions and carved out alternative spaces in universities, government, and global policy summits; they

---

[9] Taussig, M. T. (1980/2010) *The devil and commodity fetishism in South America.* Chapel Hill: The University of North Carolina Press.

trained successive generations of scholars to do meaningful research, teach, and build programs to educate others about the dangers posed by the forces at work transforming society. While these efforts to reform universities had powerful effects on discourse, nevertheless, the universities themselves (particularly public universities in the global North and South) have also succumbed to the logics and vagaries of the new economic order—slowly evolving, shifting, and disintegrating through years of austerity and neglect. Nowadays, across the United States, for instance, university enrollment is dropping, and many are concerned about its implications for a knowledgeable society that understands its past, present, and potential future.

Yet academic scholarship and university work were not the only labor this generation has been dedicated to. In other cases, scholars once trained in the university would seek alternative means to contribute intellectually and practically, joining various movements, aligning with work happening in communities in villages and neighborhoods, fostering grassroots educational processes, and establishing organizations and networks at the local and regional scales. They would seek to fill the gap between theory and practice in making other peaceful, cooperative, and prosperous worlds possible against the odds. Not all of these scholars would come from the field of development studies, nor even from the global North, but from other fields and places, drawn into the ranks of those anxiously concerned with the massive changes imposed by the global economic order and their dehumanizing consequences.

One of these young people was a physicist born in Tehran, Iran, in 1941. His name was Farzam Arbab. Completing his doctoral degree from the University of California, Berkeley, in 1968 with a focus on subatomic particles, he followed a very unconventional path compared to his peers who graduated from that prestigious program associated with seven Nobel Prizes and such names as Robert Oppenheimer and Donald Glaser. Instead of pursuing a path to industry or setting up his own particle physics lab at a university in North America or Europe—a path easily open to him—he took a fellowship with the Rockefeller Foundation's University Development Program, moving to Colombia in 1969.

What would drive a young scientist—dedicated to studying the composition of atoms and the smallest elements of the universe—to move to Cali, Colombia, to support the development of scientific education and then, over time, to commit himself to advancing education, research, and development in one of its poorest regions, Norte del Cauca? Why not take advantage of the pedigree afforded him by the excellence he reached in his field and set up a laboratory in the most prestigious North American or European higher education institutions? Similar questions come to mind when we consider a similar decision made by George Washington Carver, one of the greatest chemists of his generation, to turn down a lucrative position with Bell Labs in New York City.[10] So convinced was he by the vision of Booker T. Washington and his own faith and sense of purpose that, instead, he would join the agricultural sciences school of the Tuskegee Institute in 1896: a school he would then direct for the next 47 years—uplifting countless Black youth and accompanying innumerable Black farming families to regenerate agriculture, combining traditional techniques and modern science in a region dominated by the ruling plantation elites and their social networks.[11]

Farzam, then just 28 years old in 1969 and newly married, would depart the United States—following his faith and sense of purpose—to the epicenter of the Colombia sugarcane plantation system. There in Cali, he would join a group of interdisciplinary social and physical scientists who, together, longed to address the challenges posed by the new orders being imposed and to transform university education for a new generation of Colombian youth—particularly Black rural youth, the grandchildren of slaves in the Cauca Valley. His words on the objective conditions created by the changes wrought by the global economic order are as fresh today as when he wrote them in the late 1990s. In an essay published in 2000, Farzam expounded on what he came to see as the reason for the disintegration of rural life:

> A most disturbing fact about the present disintegration of rural life is that it is a direct result of policy. Beliefs that predict and applaud the rural-urban trend are self-fulfilling for they are translated into strategies that impoverish the countryside and increase urban problems, thus absorbing more and more resources and accelerating the cycle. Colonialism transferred to the emerging cities of the South the abhorrent conditions that characterized so many European cities at the dawn of industrialization. Five decades of development have brought about the multiplication and growth of these cities whose problems seem insurmountable, despite the combined efforts of thousands of institutions toiling indefatigably to overcome them.
>
> But the victims of these erroneous policies are not only the broken families living partly in the village and partly in the slums of the city. The entire planet has suffered from its infatuation with a certain brand of industrialization and urbanization, as its leaders and policymakers, following their dreams and living in islands of prosperity, have lost touch both with the soul of the masses and with nature. Their relentless pursuit of what they have defined as

---

[10] White, M. M. (2018) *Freedom farmers: Agricultural resistance and the Black freedom movement.* Chapel Hill: The University of North Carolina Press.

[11] Ibid.

progress is not sufficiently influenced either by the power of rigorous scientific inquiry or by the spiritual insights of religion.[12]

While Farzam's assessment of the problem offers numerous insights explored further in this book, his overriding concern was not being right or proving this point by adding to the evidentiary record—as many of his contemporaries had done and were doing. Many in his generation had already proven with great erudition the sources and consequences of the profound changes taking place across the world. His concern was not proving with greater accuracy what the problem was but figuring out what to do about it, practically, with the communities most affected. Indeed, by the time he published this article in 2000, he was 59 years old and had been connected for 30 years to rural communities, building educational processes that enabled rural youth to become protagonists of development processes in their own communities. As he would write in the same essay:

> …I find it difficult to believe that a mature humanity will live under the conditions we define today either as urban or as rural. What seems to me indispensable is the creation of a viable future for the vast number of villages in the world, so that their dwellers can participate meaningfully in the building of a world civilization.[13]

The words emphasized in Farzam's commentary align clearly with what would become his life's work and the work of the collaborators who established FUNDAEC, La Fundación para la Aplicación y Enseñanza de la Ciencia (Foundation for the Application and Teaching of Science): creating conditions through which the world's youth, particularly rural youth from marginalized communities, could participate in social action to serve and promote the well-being of the communities in their region of the world.

These preoccupations were not just some philosophical exercise or passing intellectual fad; rather, they were tied inextricably with the lived realities of Afro-Colombian youth in the villages transformed by the sugarcane complex in the Cauca river valley when he arrived in 1969. Farzam was not concerned that some percentage of these youth get a university education, move to the cities, enter the modern industrial workforce or agribusiness sector, and abandon the farms and communities of their ancestors—as was envisaged by many at the time. Farzam's was a deeper concern. From his vantage point in Norte del Cauca, he witnessed rural Afro-Colombian and indigenous

---

[12] Arbab, F. (2000) 'Promoting a discourse on science, religion, and development' in Harper, S. (ed.) *The lab, the temple, and the market: Reflections at the intersection of science, religion, and development*. Canada: IDRC; Europe and the United States: Kumarian Press.

[13] Ibid.

communities and many villages and rural peoples caught in the grip of the newly imposing order. His disquiet was toward "the wealth of talent that went uncultivated, together with the dreams of noble futures that were unfulfilled, as injustice systematically blocked the development of potentialities."[14] His wings would not be caught in the winds blowing him further and further away from the root of the problem. He and his collaborators, other youth in Colombia like Gustavo Correa, who would help establish and lead FUNDAEC for many years to follow, remained firm and focused. FUNDAEC—the institution they would create together to contribute to unlocking the human potentialities of entire generations—would not deviate from its mission for the next 50 years. The history of this institution, the story of FUNDAEC, is the story told in the pages to follow.

FUNDAEC has dedicated itself, for 50 years, to modeling an approach to education and development that seeks to rebuild the essential relationships between individuals, groups, institutions, communities, and the natural environment within regions across the world. FUNDAEC rejected the view of development as purely tied to economic growth: a transactional exchange from the "developed" to the "underdeveloped"; as acts of charity and service-provision from one group to another; or, even further, as a technical package of solutions devised by experts from the outside. FUNDAEC's collaborators started from the essential purpose to foster universal participation in a process of learning-in-action that contributes to the well-being of the communities and regions in which its initiatives are unfolding.

Among students today, reading this text in far-flung places like rural communities in Colombia, Uganda, India, or the United States—I hope some find inspiration in Farzam and Gustavo's anxious concerns and desire to dig in and stand firm to change the fortunes of the next generations, where you reside. Indeed, how Farzam articulates the challenge of confronting the barriers that limit potentialities closes the gap through the generations. We might consider the same concern from the standpoint of George Washington Carver reaching Black youth across the southern United States in the decades following the end of slavery and the rollback of gains by freed slaves in the Reconstruction era through Jim Crow laws and segregation. What limited their potentialities? What kept them from staying? What, instead, forced them to join the Great Migration to the cities and slums of the US North, cities and towns that now, after two generations, have become the US Rust Belt?

We can consider the same anxious concern in our present circumstances globally, with the youth of today walking into classrooms

---

[14] Ibid.

with the weight of the world on their shoulders. What noble futures are being unfilled, and what is blocking them? The concern Farzam raised in the early 1970s in Colombia remains as fresh as it was then and perhaps even more urgent. To reckon with the implications of his words—the development of potentialities blocked by systematic injustice—not only speaks for the past generations of the 1960s and 70s, or of the 1890s for that matter, but the present generations, those of previous centuries, and everyone in-between.

Here, we see many people across the generations standing in the breach of the last 50 years and dedicating themselves, asking hard questions, and calling on us to answer them: How do we unblock and release the potentialities of generations of youth and adults to build another world? How do we regain a sense of our humanity? How can we bring joy to others and create vibrant communities based on cooperation, solidarity, and mutual assistance? How do we overcome the sense of superiority, competitiveness, and disregard we show one another in the modern world? How can we build a society on a firmer foundation? Indeed, upon what foundations can we build such an endeavor?

Weaving a Fabric of Unity

This book, *Weaving a Fabric of Unity*, seeks to shed light on the historical, conceptual, and methodological aspects of FUNDAEC's unique and alternative approach to the work of development practice: the releasing of human potentialities. The story herein attempts to provide access to some of the key intellectual and practical wisdom from voices that shaped FUNDAEC's evolution from its early days in the Norte del Cauca region in the 1970s (then led by a small group of youth) to the creation of a systematic educational process designed to raise individuals and communities dedicated to the promotion of community well-being. Today, these education for development programs have reached hundreds of thousands of young people in Colombia and Latin America and spread their reach to rural communities in 17 additional countries across the globe.

At a time when development thought was driving the world to adopt values and logics aligned with its desired economic order, with materialist values like individualism, competition, and control, FUNDAEC's founders had a different vision of development that was highly attentive to the collective moral values, and the spiritual and religious beliefs of the people of the world. Though perhaps unusual to those trained in the traditions of Western secularism, in the 1970s, FUNDAEC embraced and was inspired by the ever-present spiritual realities shaping thought and action amidst everyday life in rural communities. In places like Norte del Cauca, spiritual realities empowered Black and Indigenous communities to endure and maintain their sense of dignity and self-worth under conditions of oppression.

For FUNDAEC, the people's moral values and religious beliefs were not backward—as some believed—but rather valid forms of knowledge and foundational elements of purposeful individual, family, and community life. FUNDAEC embraced an ennobling spiritual mode of comprehension that contrasted with the dominant economic mode of comprehension transforming the world. Therefore, rather than shying away from or dismissing the question of moral values rooted in a more-than-materialist conception of reality, now decades later gaining traction in some circles as an essential aspect of decolonial thought and practice, FUNDAEC's efforts starting in the 1970s, as a development institution, created conditions for social action where communities could consider their spiritual and material concerns simultaneously.

Beginning in Afro-Colombian communities in Norte del Cauca, FUNDAEC established development processes focused on action research, moral leadership, and practical service that embraced diverse knowledge systems and raised the capacity of local populations to advance community well-being in the places where they lived. The educational processes they designed and facilitated, combining spiritual principles and scientific knowledge, focused essential attention on replacing existing relationships characterized by domination, competition, extraction, and destruction in their communities with relationships characterized by collaboration, cooperation, reciprocity, solidarity, and harmony—qualities that are essential to promoting shared prosperity.

FUNDAEC's efforts were not ephemeral. Their projects did not simply respond to donor-driven initiatives that came and went. At a time when the concept of rural education provided to marginalized communities was just emerging, FUNDAEC's approach, philosophy, and results contributed to changes in the rural education policies of the Colombian Ministry of National Education. As a result of these interactions with the Ministry, in the late 1970s, a resolution was announced that would open the doors to educational innovations, allowing FUNDAEC's programs and, later, other educational initiatives to reach hundreds of thousands of students in the most remote areas of the country. Over time, these rural education efforts would be adopted in other countries, serving diverse populations that lacked access to quality education.

Subsequently, FUNDAEC's Tutorial Learning System (SAT) was recognized as a valid rural education alternative by the Ministry of National Education of Colombia, was adopted by the Ministry of Education of Honduras, and used by educational institutions in Guatemala, Nicaragua, Brazil, and Ecuador, elements of which were later replicated in Uganda, Kenya, Zambia, India, and Papua New Guinea through the Preparation for Social Action (PSA) program. The SAT and later the PSA offered great opportunities to access high-quality secondary education, reaching thousands of young people in rural communities and preparing them to promote development initiatives in their own regions.

The initiatives supported by FUNDAEC did not begin or end with words, nor were they confined to the four walls of any classroom. In its history, FUNDAEC's educational processes supported the formation of action research teams with community participants to create innovative solutions to cross-cutting problems of rural development. Participants involved in FUNDAEC's educational processes developed comprehensive agroecological farming methods, poultry and pork production systems, rural teacher training programs, solidarity credit funds, seed banks among farmers, experimental plots with farmers, beekeeping projects and aquaculture, warehouses and community markets, processing of primary products to give them added value, peasant associations, and family gardens.

The learnings from these projects, significant in their own right, were finally compiled and introduced into one of the most innovative curricula in rural development, a series of some 80 texts that make up the content of the SAT and PSA programs. This content prepares people for social action in integrated development, taught through a tutorial learning system—tutors, texts, and community-based groups Additionally, FUNDAEC would establish the University Center for Rural well-being, which would offer undergraduate and graduate programs in rural education, education for social development, agricultural education, and strengthening local economies.

The challenge that FUNDAEC has dedicated itself to addressing in these 50 years is how to effectively cultivate, organize, and sustain processes of learning in action through which the population of a region can participate in the generation and application of knowledge. Furthermore, FUNDAEC has been concerned with fostering initiative among local populations to work collectively to apply that learning to achieve higher levels of spiritual and material well-being without sacrificing the well-being of present and future generations. The vision of the founders of FUNDAEC, therefore, was to train generations of young people capable of carrying out this effort and creating a social space: what Gustavo Correa has described as "a space where people can come together to produce and distribute the types of knowledge necessary to build vibrant communities." In these decades, FUNDAEC has fulfilled the promise of its founders, building a vast and growing network of people capable of helping their families, neighbors, coworkers, and collaborators to facilitate a path of self-managed development based on mutual support, cooperation, and unity. These groups or nuclei of collaborators who study, act, reflect, and consult together are considered by FUNDAEC as the basis upon which we can rebuild what we have lost and forge a better future.

Introduction

*Our collective efforts have woven a fabric of unity so resilient
that its strength resonates with us even today, rallying us
around the noble cause of the development of our region.*

Gustavo Correa

On May 11, 2022, just as many around the world began to emerge from lockdowns, social distancing, and deep reflection on our health and well-being during the years of the global pandemic, a humble gathering of friends, collaborators, and coworkers took place in a small town to the south of Cali, Colombia. Delayed by two years due to the dangers posed by the coronavirus, the gathering had assembled at the Baháʼí House of Worship just a few minutes drive south of Puerto Tejada. The group, arriving by bus, car, bike, and motorcycle, had come to pay their respects to those special souls who had, in the course of their lives, made important contributions, big and small, to the well-being of the people of the rural region in which they called home, Norte del Cauca.

Norte del Cauca is a rural area south of the large metropolitan center of Cali, Colombia. A beautiful, biodiverse, and earthly-rich region of Colombia, Norte del Cauca is one of seven subregions of Cauca, composed of the municipalities of Santander de Quilichao, Buenos Aires, Suárez, Puerto Tejada, Caloto, Guachené, Villarrica, Corinto, Miranda, Padilla, Jambaló, Caldono and Toribio, with a population of nearly 450,000. The people of Norte del Cauca principally trace their ancestry to Afro-Colombian and indigenous lineage whose cultures have shaped the region for centuries. During the last five decades, traditional agriculture and family farming in Norte del Cauca—the principal source of livelihood in the region—has been radically transformed by extensive monoculture sugarcane development inspired by Green Revolution technology, displacing ancestral indigenous and Afro-Colombian agro-ecological production methods. The erosion and fertility loss of traditional farms of the people in the region has led to decades of livelihood insecurity—a generalized vulnerability for families across

Norte del Cauca as they seek farmwork, domestic and informal work, or move to find their fortunes in the city of Cali. But, Norte Caucanos are proud of their traditions, and the resilience of their spirit is palpable even through the turmoil they have experienced over centuries past to present.

Upon arrival, the participants walked—some alone and others in pairs—up the paths leading to the Bahá'í House of Worship, where they joined together in prayer and to remember the lives of friends who had passed on. It was, for all, a precious moment long anticipated. It had been more than 45 years since these friends and coworkers first began their journey together in service to the community. Some had been lost along the way but never forgotten. These souls included Farzam Arbab, Alfaro Mina, Aldemar Valencia, Edmundo Gutierrez, Eldanurth Mina, Francineth Castro, Habib Rezvani, Hernan Mena, Javier Marín, Leonardo Laredo, Leonilde Mazabel, and Teofilo Gutierrez. There were tears and smiles, joy and sorrow, heartfelt emotions quietly held in the collective embrace of a silent moment together, sitting side by side, remembering the roads they had walked together and what they had learned along the way. This simple occasion, in many ways, marked the beginning of the end of a 50-year cycle of intergenerational action, reflection, and learning set in motion by the protagonists of FUNDAEC—the globally renowned development institution founded in 1974 by a group of young collaborators in this place, Norte del Cauca.

The most treasured guests attending the gathering included the graduates of FUNDAEC's first educational programming: its pioneering group of Promoters of Community Well-being—the Ingenieros (the engineers). The Ingenieros, as they are respectfully and affectionately called, were the first young people in Norte del Cauca to answer the call of FUNDAEC and collaborate with and lead action-research teams. They were the first to adopt its research, learning, and action approach in service to the development of their region. Nearly 50 years since they had taken their first steps with FUNDAEC, here on this day, they had returned to honor their alma mater for its profound effects on the region and to reaffirm their commitment to serving and continuing to raise another generation of youth who could carry the mantle of this noble work to which they dedicated their lives.

After the moment of quiet remembrance, the group—composed of generations of collaborators who established the first center of learning created by FUNDAEC—reconvened in a circle in the shade of an open-air veranda surrounded by lush trees. Old friends and new ones mingled and spoke to one another. Young people and elders showed one another great respect. It was there, in that circle in time and space, that Gustavo Correa—the first director of FUNDAEC, appointed and entrusted by its founders to direct the initiative in 1974 at the young age of 27—stood before the group of his former students, now, at 74 years of age. Reminiscent of that moment in *100 Years of Solitude* when Ursula realizes that time was not passing but rather turning in a circle, Gustavo, in tones of a loving friend, reminded those assembled of the road they had walked together: the history and origins of FUNDAEC, its key concerns, its central principles, its inspiration, and the urgency of the continued work of strengthening the vision and practice of development in Norte del Cauca. We draw upon his words, as he shared them that day, to set the tone for the book you are reading, to welcome you into the circle of time, and to provide a glimpse into the context for the conversation that will progressively unfold in the pages to follow.

Gustavo Correa addressing participants gathered at the Baháʼí House of Worship in Norte del Cauca to reflect on nearly five decades of FUNDAEC's efforts in the region, May 11, 2022

Ingenieros, along with staff and friends of FUNDAEC, participating in the May 11, 2022 gathering

Gustavo Correa

Nearly 50 years have elapsed since we first joined forces to learn together, deliberate, and undertake projects that would contribute to the progress of the people of Norte del Cauca. Our collective efforts have woven a fabric of unity so resilient that its strength resonates with us even today, rallying us around the noble cause of the development of our region. Despite the diverse paths life has presented to each of us, our shared dedication continues to define and unite us, enabling a dialogue among friends that feels as fresh and immediate as if we had parted just yesterday. Hence, we will not confine today's gathering to any formal structure; it is, rather, an informal and heartfelt conversation among long-standing colleagues.

In the 1970s, when we started, we were at a very critical time in the path of societal development. At that time, many believed that one of the world's most pressing problems, food production, was on the way to being solved through advanced agricultural technologies. The concept and program of the Green Revolution had emerged, with major international agricultural research centers beginning to offer technological packages to address the global food issue. Many argued that ensuring the food supply for the entire world's population would allow other efforts to focus on advancing other areas and aspects of social development. However, this solution was in line with the predominant economic growth model. The assumption was that progress and development were synonymous with unlimited economic growth in both production and consumption. Even though some voices pointed out the need to recognize the limits of endless growth and respect the resources provided by nature, the proponents of this model chose to ignore such considerations.

With the passing of the years, over several decades, the signs from nature have become increasingly forceful, unequivocally indicating that our planet has limits and that we have been crossing dangerous thresholds. We are reaching a point where continuing with the same model is extremely risky. This model has persisted, acquiring an array of disguises over time, camouflaging itself under different terms. However, at its core, it has not undergone significant changes; it remains essentially the same. During the 1970s, voices began to question the path followed until then. However, those promoting this model silenced these voices. Among the questioning voices were the advocates of appropriate technology and the concept of 'small is beautiful.' They questioned the necessity of gigantism and argued that economic efficiency could also be achieved with 'apparently' more modest approaches.

In the context of these discussions, we formed FUNDAEC, an organization that stood out precisely for creating alternatives to the dominant development model—despite its magnitude and power. Our ideas originated from a different perspective on development. The organization advocated for a deeper understanding of the limits of nature and the value of more holistic and sustainable approaches. Its actions had to harmonize with the environment, focusing on liberating all human potential while avoiding the pursuit of unbridled economic growth.

FUNDAEC collaborators were deeply concerned that a purely materialist conception of the world distorted our understanding of development and ignored essential moral dimensions. Concerned about the value systems that guide the dominant development model, we turned to spiritual and religious traditions—these established sources of moral direction provided us with essential principles and guided us toward a renewed vision of development. The teachings of the Bahá'í Faith and the writings of Bahá'u'lláh, due to our close connection to them, served as the foundation for developing FUNDAEC's guiding principles and conceptual framework. Those of us who were Bahá'ís among the initial contributors regarded these writings as a Divine Revelation for our time. Other members of our group, who did not share our beliefs, viewed Bahá'u'lláh's writings as the work of a great thinker who provided teachings relevant to our era. These writings offer a promising vision of the world and a reinvigorated purpose toward a new social order. They explain the shortcomings of the present order as a stage in human and social evolution, exalt the nobility of the human being, reveal the powers with which humans have been endowed to contribute to a world in continuous progress, and present fundamental principles for constructing a new order.

One of the most fundamental principles that inspired us was the oneness of humanity. From this principle, we derived our vision and many of our approaches. It helped us perceive the world differently and reinterpret reality. The principle of the oneness of humanity invites each individual to reexamine how they see themselves: as oppressed or privileged in society or as someone with a deep social and human responsibility towards all inhabitants of the planet. The concept of the oneness of humanity influences the way we perceive others: instead of seeing people according to their social status, skin color, gender, origin, or language, we approach all people as beings with souls, where equality is paramount. It also highlights that each individual "is like a mine rich in gems of inestimable value" and that we exist to transform this world, to turn it into a place where peaceful, harmonious coexistence is possible and where justice and unity shine.

The principle of oneness also helped us acquire a sense of life's organic nature, allowing us to perceive the landscape as an integrated whole: people, communities, industry, mining, agriculture, forests, and rivers. By striving to understand the different components and practicing the art of visualizing these parts as an organic whole, we learned to identify and transform our interactions with the world and each other. The harmful relationships of domination, exploitation, extraction, and competition, which consume, isolate, and separate, were replaced by beneficial relationships of love, empathy, cooperation, and mutual aid, which bring people closer, unite them, build communities, and make collective projects possible and successful. With the principle of oneness and other fundamental principles and concepts, we built an evolving conceptual framework to provide consistency and guide our efforts.

Access to knowledge and the generation of new knowledge from our projects occupied an important place in our initial considerations. We understood the importance of not only technological knowledge but also scientific knowledge—so necessary for meaningful participation in the development process. We recognized science as a faculty of human beings that allows them to investigate the mysteries of nature and stimulate their creativity. In our comprehensive conception of development, religion and science were in continuous dialogue and complemented each other, helping us to identify the challenges of development and their causes and propose strategies and lines of action consistent with the agreed principles. From these and other deliberations, and this convergence between the material and the spiritual, FUNDAEC was born. Led by Farzam Arbab, who had a solid scientific background and spiritual perception, a group of people began to explore how to apply scientific and spiritual knowledge to accompany the population of Norte del Cauca on their path of development.

This understanding led to one of FUNDAEC's main tasks: education. We set out to ensure that a significant number of people developed the set of scientific and technological capabilities necessary to be promoters of the development of their own communities. These capabilities enabled them to lead learning processes about different aspects of social and economic life, be agents of local projects and initiatives, and serve as liaisons and mediators with regional entities and organizations. We were convinced that it would be very difficult to advance what we had proposed without genuine access to knowledge and the development of individual and collective capacity. With this understanding, we created FUNDAEC's central focus: education for development, which led to the definition and articulation of various learning programs. It is important to highlight that FUNDAEC adopted an integrated but not religious perspective. FUNDAEC is not a religious institution but a development entity that includes the spiritual dimension in its scientific approach to reality, awakening and activating the powers born from the human spirit.

FUNDAEC's educational content, developed throughout its history, reflects its conceptual framework's principles, concepts, and beliefs through a pedagogy that constantly promotes inquiry, reflection, and analysis. These materials also serve as a historical archive that documents experiences and participation in the processes of community life in Norte del Cauca. Its pedagogical approach facilitates participants in its educational programs to internalize essential knowledge while contributing to the well-being of their own community. The concept of capacity allows for the integration of technical, mathematical, scientific, and language skills within the context of a region but from a broader perspective that includes both the national and global spheres. The principle of the oneness of humanity guides students to view the world integratively, fostering a lifelong commitment to service to the community. This commitment has become the hallmark of participants in all FUNDAEC programs and a distinctive feature of their identity. Community service is, indeed, the central pillar of all our educational programs.

Today, after almost 50 years, we can clearly appreciate what we have achieved together. We have contributed in several crucial aspects to the development of the region: we have strengthened the local economy through the promotion of small businesses, productive projects, and local markets; we have raised environmental awareness in the region and transformed the landscape by planting thousands of trees that reflect native diversity and help recover endangered species; we have created a mother food forest that we hope to replicate in many communities; we have enriched the body of agricultural and livestock knowledge in the region, which now extends to the regenerative agriculture farm in Perico Negro and many other local farms; and we have trained a number of young people as promoters of development in their own communities. Finally, the people and institutions that, in one way or another, are linked to some of the FUNDAEC programs have formed an increasingly extended network. Through this network, information about local, regional, and national initiatives, the progress of collective projects, new knowledge and findings, and displays of affection and appreciation among participants circulate in all directions.

Today, gathered once again, we must celebrate these achievements and reaffirm our convictions. It is time for each of us to reexamine our role in this emerging movement, whose voice is growing louder. This movement, started by those present here, has been growing with the support of new generations of conscious people who contribute daily to this noble cause of development.

Interlude

After some moments following Gustavo's words, the veranda was quiet, and the breeze and the birds became noticeable again in the air.

The friends in the circle began to adjust in their seats, moved by his words, reminded of the road they had walked together. Then, one by one, each of the Ingenieros broke the verbal silence with testimony about the changes the community endured, the role of FUNDAEC in unlocking their potential and the human potential of their generation, and the urgent need to continue and recommit themselves to the work of transforming Norte del Cauca to reflect the aspirations of its inhabitants. Here, we provide several testimonies as evidence of the beauty and power of the words of the previous generations to urge us forward. These words demonstrate the desire of the Ingenieros, the desire of their generation, to continue working for a better world for future generations.

Rosa María Orejuela

Good morning to all. My name is Rosa María Orejuela, and I am from the youngest municipality in Colombia, Guachené. I am also from the first graduating class of FUNDAEC. I will tell you some things that have been very important in my life. But before that, I want to thank Almighty God, Mother Nature, life itself, my family, my parents, and you, my teachers, who helped me build my life. I arrived at FUNDAEC in 1974—but don't do the math (laughing). When I arrived at FUNDAEC, I had a three-year-old baby.

I remember that in Guachené, the markets are on Mondays, and I went to buy potato chips. There, Maritza Mancilla told me, "Do you want to study? A man has arrived looking for young people to study." And I told her, "Liar, why do you tell such lies? People don't come and look for you to study with them." But Maritza said, "Come, I will introduce him to you." Maritza introduced me to Gustavo Correa.

Gustavo was sitting on a bench around a wooden table. I was coming from the square to buy some socks for my baby, and I said to him, "Sir, good morning." He replied politely, "Good morning, sit down." He took out a sheet of paper from his math text with a numerical problem to solve. When I solved it, he asked me, "Would you like to be included in an educational program?" Gustavo, don't you remember? When he told me I could be included, my heart jumped with joy, and I went looking for my mother. I told her, "Mom, I'm going to study. But don't worry, you don't have to invest money there. We do not have to pay, and they will provide food."

I had an ugly suitcase. I packed as much as I could into that thing with all my joy. I put the suitcase on my head like this (making an upward motion with her arms), like putting a jar on your head when you go out to collect water. And they said, "Rosita, where are you going?" I left that day. I didn't know what I was doing, but I left walking through Guachené, San Jacinto, La Dominga, El Crucero de Gualí, and I arrived at La

Arrobleda. When I arrived, I met a lady who had also traveled there to cook for us, Doña Leo. And I said, "Madam, hello, I am included in the study program: where am I going to sleep?" And she told me, "Ah, yes, yes yes," and placed me in a cabin with everything I needed. They gave me a glass of milk, but I was not used to drinking milk, so it made me feel a bit sick, but that's another story.

When we started, I went to the field with Arnubio, another colleague who had experience with rice cultivation. He said to me, "What do you know about rice?" I told him, "No, nothing, but I am ready to learn; let's get started." I began studying and put my heart and soul into all the materials FUNDAEC gave us: community service, descriptions, mathematics, and health. I loved it a lot. But it was also a struggle, as I was a single mother.

I have this intense feeling sometimes: I don't know what would have happened to me if I had not trained at FUNDAEC (now crying, sobbing). What would have become of my life? I carry this in all my heart because there was nothing more for me, especially as a single mother. It was FUNDAEC. I say this because there are still new young people who have to know that they have to struggle and put their desire into learning. They must have the will to know and struggle because the betterment of our community is out there; it is possible. We're just getting started.

In the morning hours, I wrote down some words inspired by FUNDAEC and my teachers that I want to read to you all: "Life has no manual. We build the manual ourselves to understand what we do step by step. We build the family we want. We build the region we want. The human being is not a container to fill. She is a being with capabilities that allow her to develop herself and the environment in which she lives." That is what FUNDAEC did. This is what we learned. FUNDAEC transformed us to say to the members of our community: "Hello, how do you feel? If there are problems, how can I help you? If you have an interest in serving others, then let's develop together and move forward."

With the years I have left, I feel very strengthened and very blessed by God. I got breast cancer about two years ago, but here I am in control and fighting it. Believe me. On September 25, 2020, I was preparing a meal when I opened my cell phone, and it said, "Death Farzam Arbab." I held onto the phone, crying and asking God why. I was crying loudly in the house, and some women there came and asked me, "What happened, Rosita?" and I said, "My teacher died." This caused me such sadness that I didn't know what to do.

Gustavo, Haleh, and others: We can't stop. This seed must continue to grow. I have 12 grandchildren. I came into the world to serve them, too. So I don't know what we are going to do. I started to think about my children's and my grandchildren's education; what would it be like?

Gustavo, this cannot end. This development, this moral development, this spiritual development, technological development, professional development, this growth of science, and so on. FUNDAEC must continue to grow to foster transformation in Norte del Cauca and elsewhere for future generations.

Maricela Viveros

I was conversing with my friends here, and they told me that our young people are losing hope due to all the negative forces harassing society today. But then I told him: "Think about us, the 23 Ingenieros working together from the beginning, attacking all those problems that existed at that time in the Norte del Cauca." If we had stayed together, perhaps the situation would not be so serious now, right? But as we have already mentioned, we took different paths. Now, we must see what we can do from these different paths. I stayed on the education side with the Bahá'ís of the region. During these years, I have worked with many children and young people in practically this entire region. Unfortunately, because efforts must be made here and there, there is no systematic way to advance faster.

Despite the world's decline, we can see hopeful things happening. When we arrived in the community with the FUNDAEC programs, there were only four technicians, including a few students from SENA (Servicio Nacional de Aprendizaje). Now, the community has 104 people, including professionals, technicians, and masters. Truly, this produces a lot of joy, and we see progress.

For example, one community group works with disabled people and their families to establish home gardens. Right now, we have 35 families benefiting from the project, and at the same time, they are educating their children and talking about their children's education in those spaces. Also, the farmers now, who are the people with whom we worked in the past when some agricultural technologies were introduced in Alegrías, have managed to be independent. Initially, they earned their living by working for their neighbors, but they began to work their lands little by little. In Alegrías now, everyone is working on their land. So, I think we made progress. We must see how we continue to grow and project all that outward, and we still have much to learn. But I think the spiritual part developing in the community has been foundational. Now, there is more trust. We are discussing creating a community bank because there is already trust among the people who have developed the necessary qualities to carry out that project.

Alirio Sanchez

I want to highlight something fundamental in FUNDAEC: awakening consciousness. I don't know what others call it, but it is awakening consciousness of the capacity to serve others. If I am well and my neighbor is ill, the town will not grow, and the quality of life will not improve. We achieve quality of life when we all work from the bottom and raise our level by improving the community environment. I think we have improved the quality of life. FUNDAEC awakened that in us, service to the community. If my neighbor is doing badly, I am doing badly. And that makes us all reflect. Look, the training that FUNDAEC gave us 48 years ago still exists in each of us: service for others. Unless society does not start serving each other, this situation we are in is going to continue getting worse.

Unless society begins serving each other, this is going to get worse. Our problems—health problems, education problems, global warming problems—are serious and can lead to the extermination of the human race. The pandemic stripped the world and Colombia and Norte del Cauca naked. Before, each of us lived in our own happy bubble. But when the pandemic arrived, it showed us that people who had land were still enduring hunger, which is inconceivable.

José Parmenides Mera Larrahondo

I agree with Alirio, and I have a very great concern. Look, the world is undergoing immense changes, and we are not holding hands to address it. For instance, everything that we use to produce food is with chemical fertilizers. With the war, chemical fertilizers will not reach us, and we will depend on food from elsewhere in large quantities. Today, there are a large number of people who, due to the cost of food, have had to ration, ration, ration, and my concern is in six months, if that is happening today and we had chemical fertilizer assistance in six months, what are we going to do? And the next time, what are we going to do?

What some of our colleagues said earlier about everyone having a home garden now seems praiseworthy to me. I would only add that we also have to learn to produce organically again. I believe that is what we need to create sustainability and truly ensure that people have sovereignty in this place and in any region of the world. I fear there will be a famine that will cause further social decomposition that will be desperate and uncontrollable. So we have to start thinking, getting ahead of that situation, and considering what we will present as an answer.

Arnubio Diaz Lugo

The first university in Norte del Cauca was FUNDAEC. The first university for Black communities to access high-quality education in this region. FUNDAEC is the heritage of the people of Norte del Cauca. FUNDAEC's knowledge, practicality, vision of development, and vision of a new world are in its texts; it is in the people who are still there with the fragrance of FUNDAEC, those who work at FUNDAEC. We now need to see what we have to do. Last year, we were dealing with the problem of young people in the streets, who, at the country level, rose. I started talking to young people, and what I found was bleak. When we entered FUNDAEC, we had hope. The young people today have less hope. The institution that knows how to address the problem in Norte del Cauca must fulfill its promise here with the new generation.

FUNDAEC has to continue with its education process because it is the only thing that saved us. We, who were children of campechos,[15] we who had no options. FUNDAEC raised us, and everyone started looking to us for support, looking to us to act. FUNDAEC and all of us must come out of our shells again and recommit to the people of Norte del Cauca. I say: Let the rain spoil us, let the sun hit us, and let people see us and touch us. That is the call I make to you: to continue the education process. I don't know when I'm going to die, but I want to believe that what I learned should continue to serve people. I want to continue, and my commitment is total; I am committed for life. I want to come back because here, the people of Norte del Cauca and humanity need us and need FUNDAEC.

Weaving Our Stories Together

Gustavo's and the Ingenieros' words tell an intellectual and practical story written by FUNDAEC and its collaborators throughout its life as an institution. They also urge us to contemplate the future work of raising generations who can bring about the great transformations—the peace and shared prosperity—necessary in regions worldwide today. To aid these generations, in this book, we shed light on aspects of the historical and intellectual trajectory of FUNDAEC and provide crucial context for its creative evolution through time. The chapters that follow represent a dialogue between three friends: Gustavo Correa, one of the founders of FUNDAEC and its director from 1974 to 2005; Haleh Arbab, who co-founded and served as director of FUNDAEC's University Center for Rural Well-Being from 1994 to 2005; and Bradley Wilson, the founding director of the Center for Resilient Communities at West Virginia University who has been a close collaborator with FUNDAEC. As Rosa mentioned, one thread among many that binds us together is Farzam

---

[15] A derogatory term for campesinos or peasants.

Arbab, who, though not with us in physical presence, continues to urge each of us forward with the power of his unyielding spirit—to advance these conversations and to write down our experiences, weaving this narrative together for future generations.

From left to right, the authors, Bradley Wilson, Haleh Arbab, and Gustavo Correa

A Conversational Approach

Through the conversation that unfolds between us over the remaining chapters, the book offers insights into different periods of FUNDAEC's intellectual and institutional growth. Rather than presenting a linear narrative, the reader is invited deeper and deeper into FUNDAEC's approach by progressively moving forward, like weaving on a loom, moving back and forth, pulling threads of insight together, and tightening those threads into a colorful patterned fabric chapter by chapter. The interplay of voices in the construction of the narrative advances the conversation on the basis of questions, commentaries, and reactions to each other's recollections and perspectives. We have described the structure of our dialogue as a loom, creating a framework for weaving. Using this loom, we gathered the threads and perspectives of the three who participated in the conversation, along with the added voices of other collaborators.

The idea of writing a book of lived experiences chronicling the first 50 years of FUNDAEC took shape in the past few years in conversations between the three of us, though it's unclear who first suggested we write together. Nevertheless, in the fall of 2023, we began. The book's contents emerged from conversations over several months, from September 2023 until March 2024. Each week, we agreed to a set of prompts and questions to open the dialogue, enabling us to explore key moments, experiences, processes, and concepts that shaped the arc of FUNDAEC's development from the early 1970s to the present. Every Friday, we would meet to have a conversation, and in the following week, we would read through the transcripts, refine certain ideas, and advance. As Gustavo once jokingly remarked, "We are learning, we are learning here how to write a book together."

Yet, the concept behind building the book from a series of conversations was not happenstance. Many years ago, during Haleh's postgraduate studies, she had intensively read a book edited by her friend, Sue Thatcher, which featured a conversation between Miles Horton and Pauolo Freire titled *We Make the Road by Walking: Conversations on Education and Social Change*.[16] This book emerged as a spoken dialogue between two educators who had dedicated their lives to promoting education for social transformation in Brazil and the United States. Bradley, too, during his postgraduate studies, was deeply influenced by the book and continues to teach it to his students. So when we began to meet, we agreed that this book project also be structured as a conversation.

Early in these conversations, we often asked ourselves, "Who is this book for?" Haleh remarked, "To make any intellectual or artistic work meaningful, it should speak to someone." She described how many people write memoirs to pass their stories on to their children and grandchildren. "There's a powerful urge to write to preserve memories for the future," she said. "However, this book is meant not just for the young but for anyone, at any age across the generations, who is interested in helping to build a better world."

Haleh's remarks helped us come close to answering who our audience might be. Yet, as Gustavo stated quite clearly from the outset, we did not aim to fully satisfy the curiosity, interest, or intellectual unrest of every reader interested in learning about education and development or about FUNDAEC's contributions in the field. "If one wished to delve deeper into these topics," he said, "it would be necessary to consult other sources and materials available, which are easily accessible." Indeed, these are also sources that we reference from time to time. From the prolific pen of Farzam Arbab, the main visionary of FUNDAEC, and people close to him, there are documents, publications, talks, and many educational materials at various levels. There are also doctoral, master's, and undergraduate theses, studies, and evaluations written by individuals highlighting specific topics. From this historical archive of texts, one can

---

[16] Horton, M. (1990). *We make the road by walking: Conversations on education and social change.* Temple University Press.

better understand FUNDAEC's innovations and what it has learned in implementing a particular education and development approach.

This book differentiates itself from these other texts because it gathers insights from specific moments of FUNDAEC's journey. Moreover, we have written it for current actors working in the field who deserve to hear this story narrated from a more intimate perspective and in a language close to them, which reaches not only the mind but also the heart. Knowing the history of these 50 years enlightens the path and can prevent us from repeating past mistakes. We also hope that by revealing questions and crossroads that appeared for FUNDAEC at different moments and describing how its protagonists approached them and where they found answers, both novices and the experienced may better navigate the daily obstacles they encounter as they weave their way forward.

The conversational approach to this book written by the three of us also highlights the essential value of camaraderie in any project. When we reflect on the introduction, it is clear that camaraderie has been pivotal to FUNDAEC's resilience over time. This book was not merely the product of individual intellectual work but of friendship, love, and mutual respect across generations. There were many laughs and hard memories, confidence-building, and worries that shaped the contours of our conversations. There is much to learn from a conversational approach to writing, which eschews the conventions of socially isolated knowledge production and consumption, which are common today. We hope that this style of writing calls on the reader to listen, with an open mind to the dialogue rather than jumping quickly to conclusions, and to consider how these insights might translate into their own stories, lives, and efforts.

Conversations, dialogues, and stories are also a hallmark of every educational text developed by FUNDAEC over the course of its 50 years. So, it seemed natural that we would use a consultative and conversational approach to writing this book, given FUNDAEC's pedagogy. While advancing more slowly than texts that seek to overly synthesize ideas and drive the reader to a given conclusion with haste, reading a conversation enables greater nuance and is more akin to the way we listen to one another. That said, we feel the reader will not find the conversations lacking sophistication or overly sentimental. This is no ordinary memoir. Rather, the histories, lessons learned, concepts, and weighty ideas emerge organically through stories and reflections embedded in lived experience. Furthermore, we hope that our words and ideas capture the spirit of humility with which they were shared between us in conversation, mirroring the kind of discourse more commonly observed in the process of consultation.

Lastly, the listening posture required in consultation may provide further insight into Bradley's participation. Bradley—as many inspired by FUNDAEC's vision of building centers of learning in regions across the world—has attempted to translate elements of FUNDAEC's approach in his own context, working in West Virginia. He is not alone in that endeavor. Many in the younger generations are striving to do the same. In our early conversations, he frequently noted the value of and yearning for deeper insights from FUNDAEC's protagonists, past and present. Hopefully, the kinds of prompts we created together and the questions Bradley asks along the way offer entry points to the reader as they consider how to contribute to building centers of learning and development processes where they live and serve.

The Conversational Loom

We would like to share a few more words on the book's structure and how we set up the loom to weave our conversations together. This explanation may be helpful to the reader as we break from many of the rhetorical conventions of authorship common within literature, particularly the kinds of scholarly texts one might read in the university context. Each chapter begins with a concise introductory prompt entitled "Opening." These prompts were the outcome of our consultation to determine the most important subjects to cover. Writing the prompts together was a critical task, completed prior to entering the conversations. Our recorded conversations were not just spontaneous outbursts of thought in a few chance encounters but were disciplined by these co-authored prompts.

In short, much like setting up a loom before weaving, the sections entitled "Opening" were used to frame and organize the conversations into a coherent structure to enable our weekly dialogues to work more naturally. These "openings" provided needed guides to bring us back to unity of thought—in guiding minds to a shared set of questions and unity of action—in meeting the goal of advancing the dialogue, writing, and editing for brevity or clarity. They enabled us to speak more creatively and with enough discipline to ensure that what we said was useful to the dialogue. We think these "openings" will also assist the reader to have a clearer understanding and more meaningful entry point into the purpose of the dialogue in each chapter.

After the opening of each chapter, the narrative then moves forward based on the spoken dialogue and the organic back and forth of the speakers. The speaker offering their perspective, whether it is Haleh, Gustavo, Bradley, or, in the case of later chapters, other FUNDAEC collaborators, is marked by their name at the beginning of their contributions. The reader may wish to make note of these shifts in speaker and voice from time to time. The only chapter that deviates from this structure is Chapter 5, "Releasing Human Potentialities," where, after the opening prompt and synthesis of the previous chapters, the group agreed that Haleh should elaborate on some features of FUNDAEC's approach, drawing on her experience. The chapter concludes with a synthesis that further clarifies the practice of FUNDAEC's approach to development. One additional slight deviation in the narrative is Chapter 6, where María Cristina Mosquera and Ever Rivera, leading the Growing Hope project in Norte del Cauca, join Haleh, Gustavo, and Bradley. In this chapter, Gustavo provides the historical background, and we all offer reflections on the learning process unfolding, which is leading to growth in home and community gardening, agro-reforestation, and regenerative agriculture and contributing to a greater sense of food security and sovereignty in the region.

The book is composed of six chapters. In Chapter 1, "Weaving Our Stories Together," we introduce ourselves and how we came to work with FUNDAEC. Through personal storytelling, we uncover common intentions and commitments while providing a more grounded understanding of the perspectives we individually share in later chapters. Personal stories humanize individuals, acknowledge their experiences, and deepen connections.

Chapter 2, "Textiles of Trust," explores the significance of building relationships of trust in development work concerned with releasing human potentialities. Here, we highlight FUNDAEC's approach to building genuine relationships in response to the shortcomings of traditional development and research practices. The conversation explores key concepts such as the dialogue of knowledge, distinctiveness of place, regional change, relationship building, participation, the extended family, mutual and shared commitment and the importance of modest yet persistent actions in achieving meaningful change.

Next, in Chapter 3, "Interwoven Commitments," we consider how FUNDAEC grew from the profound learning from the early period of action research in the 1970s to lay the foundation for an approach to education for development through the tutorial learning system or the SAT that would later expand to other regions of Colombia and beyond. As FUNDAEC expanded beyond Norte del Cauca, questions arose about appropriately replicating its approach in new contexts without imposing values or technologies. The organization navigated this challenge by prioritizing organic growth, ensuring that expansion did not compromise its principled intent. Decisions about scaling up initiatives were made through consultation, considering how many people and communities could benefit while maintaining the integrity of the approach through interwoven commitments forged in partnership and training.

In Chapter 4, "A Living Tapestry," we discuss FUNDAEC's transition in the 21st century, focusing on the transition period from the SAT to the Preparation for Social Action (PSA) program, which aimed to refine its approach and cultivate a new generation of Promoters of Community Well-being. This program propelled FUNDAEC onto a global path of collaboration. The conversation highlights FUNDAEC's continuous commitment to adaptation and evolution in its transformative approach to development. Central to this chapter is FUNDAEC's enduring focus on building capacity in a significant number of people to serve its programs in regions around the world.

In Chapter 5, "Releasing Human Potentialities," we synthesize the insights of the previous chapters and then turn to a commentary by Haleh Arbab that seeks to bring together key threads that shape FUNDAEC's distinctive approach to development, education, and research. She notes that weaving together this approach through language is challenging, as it encompasses a wide array of intellectual and social practices that shape the organization's behavior and outcomes. Rather than just a methodology, FUNDAEC views its approach as encompassing moral intentions, philosophical assumptions, methodological considerations, and experiential qualities that guide inquiry and action. Haleh explores how FUNDAEC's approach emerged from significant intellectual debates surrounding development, science, education, and community participation. Central to this approach is forming groups that embark on action-reflection, study, and consultation cycles, highlighting the relational nature of development, research, and education. This holistic perspective underscores FUNDAEC's commitment to ongoing, interwoven education, research, and development processes.

In Chapter 6, "Picking Up the Threads," we bring the story of FUNDAEC to the present day to see how its champions continue to fulfill its steadfast commitment to promoting food production and sovereignty in Norte del Cauca and elsewhere, drawing on diverse sources of knowledge and collaborating with local communities to promote reforestation and regenerative agriculture. The project Growing Hope, launched amidst the pandemic, builds on FUNDAEC's decades-long work to raise human resources and foster participation in processes of development at the regional scale, exemplifying its enduring hope in action for the betterment of the communities in Norte del Cauca and around the world. A special feature of this chapter is that the dialogue expands beyond Gustavo, Haleh, and Bradley to include María Cristina Mosquera and Ever Rivera, key champions of the Growing Hope project in Norte del Cauca, in the conversation.

Weaving Our Stories Together

Attachment to the land and its people is an intrinsic aspect of our humanity. I believe that the human heart has the capacity to embrace many places and many people. Having the world as our homeland means cherishing every piece of land with equal passion. Nonetheless, building and creating require dedication and unwavering commitment to a specific place. True meaning and purpose don't arise from mere drifting.

Haleh Arbab

Opening

One of the unique characteristics of FUNDAEC's approach to development is the recognition of the dignity of every human being and that each person has gifts, talents, and abilities from which our communities can benefit. Through relationship building, personal storytelling, and testimony, we can hear what moves people; we can orient one another to what unites our stories; and through listening, we can recognize each other's common intentions and commitments. By listening to stories, we also have the opportunity to question our assumptions, reach toward understanding someone else with an open mind, and perhaps gain new insight into the sense of purpose in a given endeavor. Finally, stories with ennobling themes can inspire others to undertake noble acts.

In contexts where we seek to work individually and collectively to advance the well-being of one another and the communities in which we serve, telling one's story is a natural and vital practice wherein we acknowledge people's distinctive sense of place in the world, their lived experiences, and the nature of the paths they have traveled. In simple terms, telling stories humanizes us. The goal here in introducing ourselves is more modest than this. We hope that through the following stories, the reader might feel closer to the conversation we are having together and understand better why it unfolded in the way it did. These introductions deepened the bonds of friendship, admiration, and mutual understanding.[17] Yet, they also offer insight into storytelling as a vital practice in strengthening one's sense of one's place in the world and building trust within groups accompanying one another in intellectual work and social action.

Gustavo

On many occasions, people have asked me how I became involved in the field of development, abandoning a path I had set out for myself when I decided to study mathematics, my passion during the last years of school, with the goal of becoming a university professor. Mathematics and teaching were two things that had always attracted me. I remember that one of my favorite games with my younger brothers was to "play school," where I was the teacher.

Everything seemed to favor me when, after graduating as a mathematician from the Universidad del Valle in 1973, they offered me a position as an instructor to teach basic mathematics to students entering university for the first time. But a conversation with Farzam Arbab soon after led me to a crossroads. He, an elementary particle physicist, had come to Colombia after earning his doctorate in physics from the University of California at Berkeley, to advise the newly established physics department at the Universidad del Valle. His coming was part of the support that the Rockefeller Foundation gave the university to strengthen the faculties of science and health. I had met Farzam, who had recently arrived at the university as my professor of a physics course, which turned out to be the first course assigned to him as a newcomer.

My conversations with Farzam after class were not about physics or mathematics but development. Farzam had been participating in a multidisciplinary group at the university, where they discussed strategies for—what we then called—integrated rural development. This model recognized that aspects of agricultural production, health, employment, education, and technological development are much more interconnected in the rural sector and that, therefore, the strategies to achieve development needed to use a multidisciplinary approach. Farzam told me he had also met with colleagues from other faculties, including education, to explore the best way to impart quality scientific and technological knowledge to the rural population. We discussed these issues and maintained that the only way to achieve true development was when communities actively participate and have access to technological and scientific knowledge. He invited me to join the group in that conversation, which I enthusiastically accepted.

[17] There were moments when we reconsidered the relevance of sharing these personal stories with the readers for fear that it over-personalized a book that is really the experience of the development of an institution, FUNDAEC. Yet, the basis of our dialogues together was born of mutual respect for our unique and shared experiences. Therefore we thought it was important to tell the reader some of the stories we have shared with each other.

There, I met the medical doctor Alberto Alzate, the chemist Cecilia de Plata, the physicists Edmundo Gutiérrez and Javier Marín, and others who came sporadically.

From left to right, Gustavo Correa, Javier Marín, and Farzam Arbab, 1970s

So, I began to delve, although with suspicion at first, into a field completely unknown to me. The conversations that followed and the visits for the first time to the region of Norte del Cauca to interact with the peasants and learn about their reality had to do with my decision, later on, to suspend the career that was outlined at the university and dedicate myself, together with the other colleagues, to create FUNDAEC, a legal entity separate from Universidad del Valle that gave us greater freedom than the university, to explore and validate other ideas about development.

The first years of intense learning and study required us to free ourselves from our professions in order to understand and delve into all the dimensions of rural problems, and forge a vision of what we considered an integrated approach. My knowledge of the rural sector was like that of many middle-class young people in the city at that time, whose contact with the countryside and the peasants was very superficial. Fortunately, and because of my family and religious training at that time, I had managed to overcome the class prejudices with which most viewed the rural people, and had become aware of the importance and essentiality of the farmer in the organization of the life of society.

Over time, I would interact with hundreds of farmers from different regions of Colombia and other parts of the continent, get to know them better and bring them closer to my heart. In them, I distinguished the manifest and contagious qualities of all those linked to the earth and how they relate to it. They love, care for, admire, respect, and thank it because it connects them with life, brings them joy, and gives them daily sustenance. I will always be grateful to the Norte Caucano farmers who helped me to relate to the land like them, to not be intimidated by the slightest effort, to develop sensitivity to the sufferings of others, to aspire to a state of contentment that does not indicate resignation or acceptance of the injustices of which they are victims but rather a state of soul that serves to transcend and act as a shield against the multiple difficulties that threaten their lives. Even at the risk of romanticizing the farmers from this region, I am a fervent admirer of their ancestral resilience to overcome and deal with the consequences of slavery.

Francia Valcárcel and Carlos Velásquez, FUNDAEC's Office, 1980s

Over several months in 1974, we defined a very simple structure of the newly formed organization. Perhaps because I was the youngest in the group and a recent graduate, I was asked to resign from my position at the university and dedicate myself fully to the execution and monitoring of what the group decided in its weekly meetings. With a first donation from the Rockefeller Foundation, it was possible to reinforce the original group with professionals from other fields who would provide us with a multidimensional reading of rural reality. The first to arrive were Francia de Valcarcel, an anthropologist who had just come from Bogotá, the agronomists Martin Prager and Roberto Hernández, and the educators Carmen Inés Gamboa and Ana Gonzales. With these reinforcements in the social and agronomic area, we were better prepared to understand the region of Norte del Cauca and begin some research activities to learn about some of the life processes of its inhabitants.

Martin Prager and Roberto Hernández at FUNDAEC's rural center in La Arrobleda, Cauca, 1980s

From left to right, Gustavo Correa, Carmen Inés Gamboa, Francia Valcárcel, Haleh Arbab, and Edmundo Gutiérrez, Perico Negro, 1990s

We started from the idea that we cannot conceive the development of a region as a package of solutions devised by experts from outside but rather as a process that advances towards a shared vision with the conscious and well-informed participation of the people. Our main activity during the first years focused on helping develop the skills essential for participation in two groups of young people. To provide content for the courses, we designed research projects running parallel to explore agriculture, community organization, and peasant economy with the participants. The educational texts that we produced and continue to develop over the years represent the systematization of all the results of these first investigations and those that came later to explore other life processes of the population.

Remembering my first impressions of Norte del Cauca brings to mind the mixed feelings that arose during my first visits. The majestic samanes at the entrance to Puerto Tejada make it a street of honor to the visitor, evoked by the numerous species of trees that cover the immense valley of the Cauca River, formed by two mountain ranges that begin in the south of the northern Cauca region. It flows to Cartago's outskirts in the Valle del Cauca department. That beautiful imagery, however, disappears as you enter the region's roads and perceive the accelerated transformation of the landscape that had taken place. This transformation along this beautiful geographical valley began at the beginning of the 20th century with the incursion of sugar cane and other extensive monocultures that replaced the livestock farms, smallholdings, and tropical dry forest, taking advantage of the fertility of the soil and abundance of water. These changes in land use brought with them the transformation of small owners of agricultural land into agricultural workers, the displacement of rural communities from the lands most suitable for agriculture to the hillside area, and the loss of 72% of its wetlands and 66% of its forests according to data from the Autonomous Corporation of Valle del Cauca (CVC).[18]

The effects of this transformation of land use and the cultural practices of the monocultures that surrounded it, such as aerial spraying using herbicides, burning, and infrastructure works that restricted the use of water, were reflected in the gradual loss of food sovereignty and forced insertion into the dominant economic model. The smallholdings of producers of cocoa, coffee, banana, cassava, beans, aromatic and medicinal herbs, and native flora that grew under the shade or in the company of a wide diversity of forage and timber fruit trees—the Norte del Cauca peasant farm—was losing its vitality and viability and seemed doomed to disappearance. We would associate with these farmers and look in this territory for alternative development models that would rescue the beauty of the landscape, respect biodiversity, privilege diversified land use, strengthen a local economy, and advance towards food sovereignty. For this, we would need to use the experience and ancestral knowledge of the inhabitants of Norte del Cauca together with the modern scientific knowledge that has contributed to the progress of humanity in different fields. We soon realized that we were not alone in this endeavor.

Haleh

From my early years, as a young girl raised in a small house within the heart of a bustling city—a city that has been my lifelong companion, with its lively streets, bustling intersections, and towering sycamore trees—I harbored dreams of Colombia. In August 1969, my brother Farzam, accompanied by his wife and their three-week-old baby, opted to move to Cali, a charming town nestled at the foothills of the western Andes range. Most Iranians at the time had limited knowledge about Colombia, primarily associating it with exporting commodities like sugar, cotton, and coffee. Beyond these basic facts, their awareness of Colombia's culture and geographical diversity was minimal, possibly extending to recognizing the country's significant indigenous population.

In 1973, my mother and I embarked on a journey to Colombia. We flew to Paris, obtained our visas at the Colombian embassy, and boarded a flight across the Atlantic to Bogotá, the capital city. Our enthusiasm about the new country waned when the customs agents confiscated the Persian sweets we had brought. But upon landing in Cali, our eyes naturally turned upward to behold the sky while a warm breeze, carried from the nearby mountains, gently brushed against our skin. In that very

---

[18] Corporación Autónoma Regional del Valle del Cauca (Environmental Management Group, Conservation Data Centre - CDC). Comparison of forest and wetland cover between 1957 and 1986 with delimitation of critical natural communities in the Geographic Valley of the Cauca River. Santiago de Cali. 1990. p. 8.

moment, the gloomy image that Bogotá had painted was instantly transformed into one of radiant optimism and boundless possibility.

We entered the Cauca Valley, a sanctuary of unparalleled flora and fauna. Later, I discovered that the early arrivals had proclaimed it an earthly paradise, and travelers from the 17th century had marveled at it as a realm where nature unveiled the splendor of its wonders and the enchantment of its color palette. Returning to the bustling city, I maneuvered through honking cars, assertive buses, and ever-halting taxis. However, this expansive valley, adorned with its grayish-blue sky and the unforgettable breeze wafting from its protective mountain ranges, remained etched in my memory. It was the place to which I would return countless times, the place to which I would devote myself, and where I would spend most of my life.

Many years later, the following words my brother wrote in a book he titled *The Path of Learning in Latin America: Moral Option* evoked memories of my first encounters with this land. "Close bonds of affection are not limited to relationships between people; there are other manifestations of love, such, for example, as deep feelings for the land, or the indissoluble bonds that often arise between the individual and an entire people."[19] He wrote, "When I look back on the 19 years of my life in Colombia that have contributed so much to my own formation, a host of feelings emerge in me, but I believe that, of all of them, it is love that best explains my attachment to Latin America and my hope in the future of its people."

Farzam Arbab in La Arrobleda, 1980s

As I ponder the notion of a place to exist—a place to build and make meaningful contributions—words like dedication, commitment, and perseverance spring to mind. These are how people created towns, cities, and nations. People settle, labor, and craft in one location. The recurring image accompanying these thoughts, an indelible memory, is that of my

[19] Arbab, F. (1991) *La Senda del Aprendizaje en Latinoamérica: Opción Moral.* Colombia: Editorial Nur.

brother and me standing on the porch at the entrance of the house his family had leased in the Miraflores neighborhood in Cali.

The 30-year-old man, transforming from physicist to development thinker/practitioner, asked, "What do you aspire to do with your life as you grow older? What area piques your interest?" He directed these inquiries to me, a 14-year-old Iranian girl. My simple response, "To be a writer," appeared to displease the social actor in him. "In what language do you intend to write?" a question that echoed a future I feared. It confirmed the fate of exiles—those bound to leave their homelands, those compelled to acquire new tongues, and those who felt estranged from their language and sense of belonging. Just a few years later, I departed from my homeland, and naturally, I never pursued a career as a writer.

Reflections on identity, belonging, and connections to one's homeland have been constant companions throughout my life. I've pondered numerous questions about the attachments that bind an individual to the place of their birth, their upbringing, where they acquire fragments from a culture, the norms of behavior, and the intricacies of interpersonal relationships. Is it a love for the place itself or the people that serves as the wellspring of commitment, motivating some individuals to remain steadfast in one location, even in the face of the most challenging circumstances? Is it the familiar scent of raindrops, the predictable whirling of the wind, or the sun's searing heat? Alternatively, is it the aroma of a mother's kitchen, the warmth of her embrace, or a father's gentle yet resolute support?

What is the binding force that attaches people to both the land and its inhabitants? "I have never been given to feeding romantic notions, nor could my feelings be the result of that manipulation of emotions that are sometimes done to promote patriotism"[20] are my brother's words. "I had such an influence long ago in Iran, where I was born, but I soon learned that healthy patriotism had to be managed in a context of loyalty to the entire human race." He affirms his commitment to Latin America was not based on superfluous emotions "but on a richly lived experience and on having shared with many others a vision of transformation that will contribute significantly to the construction of a new global society."

My brother firmly believed that it was a shared, enriching life experience and a collective vision of a better world that motivated people to remain, persevere through their daily trials, nurture hope, and stand tall in the face of adversity. For me, the connection has been more intricate. Whatever it is, I still experience emotions when I hear the national anthem of any country playing, observing the citizens of that nation rise and sing. Nostalgia fills me as I take in the fragrance of the season's first raindrops splashing on the asphalt roads. My father's voice,

---

[20] Ibid.

urging me to run toward him, still echoes in my memory, and I awaken with tears when I realize I may never return to the house of my birth. However, I carry with me the recollection of the cool Cali breeze that graces me every afternoon, eagerly await the blossoming of pink guayacan trees each season, and eagerly anticipate the sound of the Colombian National Anthem broadcasted on the radio every evening. Attachment to the land and its people is an intrinsic aspect of our humanity. The human heart can embrace many places and many people. Having the world as our homeland means cherishing every piece of land with equal passion. Nonetheless, building and creating requires dedication and unwavering commitment to a specific place. True meaning and purpose don't arise from mere drifting.

Bradley

I grew up far from the Cauca Valley in southern New Jersey in the United States, in a small township on the other side of the river from Philadelphia. I often say that my path to work in the field of development in Latin America started with an error in judgment by my parents when they agreed to allow me to travel to Central America from the United States as a high schooler, a teenager. My beloved Spanish teacher from Costa Rica convinced my parents that I should continue my language training abroad one summer. She arranged for entry to a language school in San Jose, and off I went. Of course, I am joking; it wasn't an error by my parents. They always encouraged me to try new things. They understood that travel experiences were crucial to learning and trusted my teacher. But that first experience in Latin America transformed me. I did not return the same person.

In 1996, I spent three weeks in Costa Rica and Nicaragua. Looking back, it was such a short period, but at 17 years old, it made a big impact. Nicaragua was just emerging from a civil war, a deep political conflict and a major economic crisis that had pulled the country apart. The people I was visiting carried deep wounds. I was learning about these realities for the first time and coming to grips with the real implications of conflict and instability. I lost that privileged innocence one might enjoy living in suburban middle-class bubbles. It was sobering. I became increasingly aware that my naïveté toward Central America's political and economic situation, particularly given the deep US involvement, was simply not an acceptable way to move through the world. Too many lives were at stake at the other end of my ignorance. There was a world of something I needed to understand. That desire to understand carried me into my college years, would shape my studies and career path, and I would return to Nicaragua again and again and again.

For the next two decades, I studied and learned about education and development in Matagalpa, Nicaragua. Matagalpa was a place and a people that profoundly shaped my understanding of development and where I created friendships that transformed my understanding of the purpose of life and service to others. Matagalpa is in the Central Highlands of Nicaragua, what many would call coffee country. Others might call it the cradle of the revolution. And still others might call it one of the last strongholds of indigenous community life. I was particularly interested in learning from agricultural cooperatives, the rural development strategies they had developed amidst a period of land reform, economic experimentation, and intensive military conflict. Now, in my early twenties I did not enter that work as naïvely as I had when I was a teenager.

It was around this time I first learned about FUNDAEC, which transformed my thinking about education, research, and development in profound ways. Unlike some who may learn about FUNDAEC as a Bahá'í -inspired organization, I simply learned about it as an institution with an alternative vision for the development of rural communities in Latin America. I clutched very closely the few pieces of writing on FUNDAEC's ideas I could find at that time in print. In 2004, I reached out to Farzam Arbab, and, though brief, his sound advice served as an important source of motivation for me to persevere through my doctoral program in geography and development studies. I reconnected with Farzam again in 2018, 15 years later, to share the fruits of what had come of my efforts and to consult on how to establish a university center for participatory research in West Virginia. Again his wise counsel and generous responses to my questions about the early years of the formation of FUNDAEC provided honest encouragement and thoughtful guidance on how to go about building such a center of learning in West Virginia.

I have lived and worked in West Virginia for more than 15 years. I am raising a family here with my wife and two girls. I, too, now feel a part of this place, trying to serve the people here, trying to contribute to a process in which groups can work together and participate in their own development, to self-determine, and perhaps to imagine and enact futures that lead to what Gustavo has called higher levels of spiritual and material well-being in their communities. But to arrive at that place, to be committed to community work, and to gain people's trust takes time. It's not necessarily easy in West Virginia, where outsiders can be looked at suspiciously or perceived as yet another person who is there to ridicule, misrepresent, or sell a false promise. Even though I trace my family roots to West Virginia through my mother, there is nothing that replaces the hard learning of living, building trust and working in the region. These are also elements of a process of development, learning the ethics of place and a people forged in particular histories.

Farzam and I remained in contact as our efforts unfolded in West Virginia until his sudden passing in the Fall of 2020. Haleh and Gustavo reached out not long thereafter in November of 2020 and the conversations that had started with Farzam continued. Haleh came to visit West Virginia in the Spring of 2021 and the horizons of our possible work together grew. Valentina Muraleedharan, then a doctoral student at WVU, and I worked together to systematize a five year reflection document on the advancement of the Preparation for Social Action program in the North of Colombia. For a year or so, 2021–2022, we had been working with the team at FUNDAEC to elaborate the study and to coordinate interviews remotely. At the time it just wasn't feasible to travel to Colombia and connect with these special places and people. In 2021 the pandemic had still ground international travel to a halt, and it just didn't seem safe to visit Colombia. But in 2022, Haleh and Gustavo decided that it made sense for me to travel and present some of the work to friends at FUNDAEC and have a consultation about the study's results. I flew to Cali from the US to consider the next steps of the research with FUNDAEC.

I remember the anticipation of flying into the Cauca Valley and looking down out the window. Looking out at the mountains and valley, I experienced a rush of emotions, a feeling like I was returning to find my soul again in Latin America, a place where I forged a piece of my life journey and shaped my understanding of the world. So, seeing the green mountains and that landscape before me on my descent, I just had this real sense of anticipation about my visit to Colombia. I knew there was going to be a lot of learning from Haleh and Gustavo both about development, but also the anticipation of being with them and meeting all the friends at FUNDAEC and just putting my feet on the ground in a place that had been so critical to my conceptual learning, and a place I had imagined for so many many years, but I had never been before. It had been some 25 years since the first time that I had read about FUNDAEC in the late 1990s as an undergraduate student. The first time I read the words: Norte del Cauca.

My first recollections of Colombia, sitting there in the passenger seat of the car, was the sugarcane. The drive from the airport to Norte del Cauca is roughly 45 minutes long, and the continuous line of sugarcane fields—cane some 8 feet tall and green and lush and jagged on either side of the road like a long corridor—continued without interruption for nearly the entire drive. I don't remember much more than that. Sitting in silence with just the hum of the wind. Watching the rows and rows of cane, a worker, trucks pulling in and out of the fields, a tractor, the smoke from the burning rising on the horizon and people busy with work. Moving about their day. I just stared, mind wandering, the minutes passing by, as the jagged green blades blurred my eyes. I was entranced but not unthinking. My mind turned and turned. Why this sea of sugarcane? Why here? What story does this landscape, this region, and this place tell?

Similar thoughts often came to mind on my travels in Nicaragua, staring out at the coffee orchards or massive cattle ranches. These are also thoughts that come to mind in my current homeplace, where traces of coal extraction, not sugarcane, are visible everywhere in the landscape. In West Virginia, you can hear the trains whistling carrying coal, the barges carrying coal floating down the river, and see the power plant smokestacks in the distance from any hill. The recreational fields where our children play are on abandoned strip mines. The supermarket, the retail stores, and the new town center are all on abandoned mines on flattened hills made low by removing coal. Sometimes, it feels like we are adapting ourselves in this place to coal rather than the industry adapting itself to us. But of course, there is more to this place than coal, even if coal may have brought many families here. West Virginia is a place where people have forged ways of life and community and served one another.

Now, back to Colombia and the first impressions, the sugarcane, the people and the sense of wonder about what I would learn about development in Norte del Cauca. It brings me back to why I was traveling to visit Haleh and Gustavo and the friends of FUNDAEC. I wanted to learn from what they had learned. Doing so meant I needed to go to the place where the founders of FUNDAEC took their first steps and reflect on a journey of some 50 years. It required an understanding of the place and the people, and of how an approach to development coalesced through many years of action and reflection, advances and setbacks, and more.

Textiles of Trust

*Our journey towards becoming true partners in the pursuit of
development in Norte del Cauca was significantly aided by our
conscious effort to combat any sense of superiority, and instead,
appreciate the wealth of knowledge present within rural
communities. We recognized the value in both the academic
training and the ancestral wisdom accumulated over
generations in these communities.*

Gustavo Correa

Opening

One of the greatest concerns of FUNDAEC and many in the
field of development has been the nature of relationships of
trust within communities or regions as they pursue higher
levels of well-being. Most development practitioners or advocates
understand this trust-building as paramount to their work. They aspire
to fulfill a deep calling to serve others and meaningfully contribute their
knowledge, skills, and effort to respond to many of the ills afflicting
communities. There is no doubt that there are many people—
humanitarians, environmentalists, educators, social activists, and
entrepreneurs—around the world who have answered this call with the
best of intentions and have worked tirelessly to advance these efforts to
improve human and environmental conditions.

Yet, trust building is not always at the center of development
practice. The global history of development is replete with stories of the
breakdown of trust and evidence of poorly conceived diagnoses and
interventions, narrowly defined and even prejudiced understandings of
problems, and the exclusion of people from participation in planning and
decision-making. Sometimes, there is a kind of short-sighted and short-
lived commitment to the places that practitioners and advocates imagine
reaching higher levels of well-being. Even today, in development
scholarship and practice, we remain entangled in questions about
practicing genuine long-term commitments to people in places rather

than just finding and applying some technocratic solution of some sort or other and moving on.

At its founding in the early 1970s, FUNDAEC's earliest pioneers were conscious of the many failed promises of development practitioners and other advocacy efforts. Therefore, they sought to embody a different approach to development; they committed to tracing a different path. That path began in Norte del Cauca, a rural Afro-Colombian region south of Cali, where the Green Revolution technologies and displacement by the sugarcane industry were transforming the society and landscape. Disenchanted by the false promise of the Green Revolution and deeply concerned with the social disintegration it was causing in families and villages, Norte del Cauca became the earliest and longest-standing place where FUNDAEC's participants sought to tread a different path: to develop its approach further and put it in practice. Fifty years later, FUNDAEC has learned much from those efforts, experiences, and people.

In this conversation, we explore together how relationships established in Norte del Cauca shaped the early formation of FUNDAEC, and its vision and practice. Essential concepts emerge from the conversation, such as mutual trust, dialogue of knowledges, openness to change, a practical and realistic approach, establishing personal connections, shared commitment, and the importance of modest yet diligent actions taken over time.

Bradley

Given FUNDAEC's 50-year history and its continued work in the region, we thought it would make sense to begin by exploring relationships with people and the place of Norte del Cauca and how that shaped the development of FUNDAEC, particularly in its earlier years and even today. It is clear from this history of the institution that it built itself on a strong foundation of trust and knowledge gained through long-term embeddedness and mutual accompaniment. How has the commitment to Norte del Cauca, to this place, these people, or this region shaped the development of FUNDAEC? Why have these relationships in Norte del Cauca thrived and lasted so long?

Haleh

Providing an entirely objective answer to how our relationships thrived in Norte del Cauca is challenging; the responses are inherently subjective. However, one answer I would offer is that this population in Norte del Cauca, despite its endured hardships, possesses a remarkable openness to change. There's a genuine willingness to take action that can benefit the region. Their authenticity is unmistakable, and their sincerity shines through in their words and actions. Despite the history of oppression, slavery, and ongoing injustices that have marred the region's past, the people of Norte del Cauca are not inherently suspicious. In making this statement, I don't mean to suggest that they lack sophistication or the ability to identify attempts to exploit or marginalize them. Instead, it indicates their capacity to distinguish between acknowledging malicious intent and safeguarding against it and the tendency to form relationships rooted in mistrust. This nuanced sensibility and openness to change contributed to one of the core principles laid down at FUNDAEC's inception, resonating well with the local population: a tacit, collective commitment to grounding our interactions in trust.

Certain conditions in the region also played a crucial role in this experience. It's a common tendency among individuals working in rural development to romanticize the conditions they encounter, often resulting in superficial solutions that barely scratch the surface of the complex problems faced by those residing in rural or marginalized areas. However, this romantic notion of a rural community isolated from the hazards of modernity and urbanization did not hold in Norte del Cauca. This region was at a pivotal juncture of change, with Cali, Colombia's third-largest city, just half an hour from Puerto Tejada, the region's urban center. Many in the community had lost their land to the sugarcane industry and had to find employment within that industry or in Cali. For instance, many women worked as domestic helpers in the city during the week and returned to their families on weekends. Over time, the population became increasingly impoverished as the sugarcane industry encroached upon every corner of the region, depleting its resources. Given these harsh realities, romanticizing the situation was impossible. The ever-present threats and risks people faced demanded a practical and realistic approach.

Gustavo

A common challenge for initiating work in a new region is establishing a meaningful relationship with the local community. From the beginning, we recognized the importance of fostering an atmosphere characterized by mutual trust and ongoing dialogue. It became evident to us that achieving this requires a foundation of respect, empathy, humility, and a genuine belief in the capacity of others. Our conscious effort to combat any sense of superiority and appreciate the wealth of knowledge in rural communities significantly aided our journey toward becoming true partners pursuing development in Norte del Cauca. We recognized the value of both the academic training we had gained at the university and the ancestral wisdom accumulated over generations in these communities.

Another vital aspect to emphasize is the nature of our relationship with the communities in Norte del Cauca. It wasn't merely an institutional connection but a profoundly personal one. We came to know each family within these communities, their challenges, their accomplishments, hardships, and progress. I distinctly recall our conscientious approach to ensuring that we did not dispatch individuals who arrived at FUNDAEC to interact with the community until they had received thorough orientation and had developed the necessary sensitivity to these considerations. This personal rather than strictly institutional bond has been vital in its longevity. It has allowed FUNDAEC to be perceived not as an external program with specific objectives but as an integral institution with a defined role in the region.

Bradley

As you described, the community's openness, the challenges they confronted, and the trust with the families and communities you established shaped the nature of your interactions with people in Norte del Cauca. You were not perceived as outsiders but accepted as part of the community. FUNDAEC became an institution responsive to and of the people in the communities. This is challenging for many of us working in development. Social differences or an unconscious sense of superiority often keep us from creating trusting relationships. In the field of development or education, sometimes our relationships with people are prefigured by a set of assumptions, goals, or timelines that determine or constrain the relationship. Something else is driving the relationships behind the scenes. For instance, in a lot of development work, there is an underlying assumption that diagnosing a set of problems must happen first. When one "goes into the community," as it is often said, one goes to diagnose problems and come up with solutions. I think this is an important distinction in what you have said here. You did not build relationships in Norte del Cauca by first going to diagnose a set of problems. You seemed to go with a truly appreciative mindset to learn and understand the social context and to connect with people.

Haleh

Yes, this, too, is an important distinction in our engagement in Norte del Cauca. In one of Farzam's unpublished talks in the early 1980s reflecting on these early experiences, he discussed what he, Gustavo, and others had learned in Norte del Cauca about the need for careful consideration of approaches that are focused on diagnosing problems.

His words reverberate through time and have encoded many aspects of how we think about development and education. His comments, particularly about diagnosis and its relationship to development, are very insightful:

> There are so many different methodologies people are using for development initiatives. Many are sensitive to participation. At the most simplistic level, these concerns about participation are critical of a top down perspective and not being sensitive to the needs of the people. Therefore, there are many forms now for assessing the needs of communities such as surveying and asking people about their needs, and even more sophisticated forms of participatory observation. Many of these are concerned with refining a process ultimately focused on diagnosis.

> But, rather than discuss here the specific instruments to diagnose, we should look critically at the very concept of needs in a wider level of social context. We must ask ourselves questions such as: "What is the philosophy underlying the concept of diagnose first and give solutions afterward? This diagnostic approach to development follows a medical analogy. Someone is sick so you diagnose the sickness and give them the medicine.

> Most methodologies in development presume this kind of approach. Is that valid? Is that something that we should work with? It doesn't mean that we throw it away but we need to understand the logics of the methodologies that are at work. What are the concepts behind diagnosis? Who is diagnosing whose condition? Who gave any one person the right to go to somebody's village and diagnose their condition. And finally come up with a list of needs that maybe they were not really aware of and say, this is their real needs?

> Is development such a simple thing that you diagnose a set of conditions, you give the technologies that solve it, and there you are? Everything will just fall into place. Who has the solution?

> Does the developed world have the solutions to the problems of the developing world? So how can we in the "developed world" get in the business of diagnosing when we don't even have the knowledge for bringing about constructive change in the developed world. As we enter the field of development we will begin by encountering things that sound very good and then we will need to further analyze them from social point of view and spiritual point of view and then come up with our own methodology.

I think, in addition to building meaningful relationships with the people of Norte del Cauca, FUNDAEC also approached the work we were doing with certain skepticism toward the idea that we were intellectually prepared to diagnose "their" problems in Norte del Cauca and come up with solutions. We did not perceive our knowledge as somehow superior. We were not comfortable with being "in the business of diagnosing." We were concerned about, as Farzam said, development approaches "that sound very good" but might not foster participation or, even worse, might have unintended negative outcomes in the long term. Our interest was creating a different approach rooted in a different conceptualization of development practice focused on a commitment to the communities that would unfold over decades. This practice and posture toward the future required something from us other than a transactional or instrumental relationship with people in a short timeframe. We needed to immerse ourselves in processes of community life for a much more extended period not afforded in development projects or short-lived research projects.

Gustavo

Haleh, drawing on Farzam's words, has expressed our concerns about the diagnosis very elegantly. I want to offer a slightly different way that we arrived at a humble posture toward our work in Norte del Cauca. As she said, although we had built relationships with the people and could appreciate the depth of their challenges, we were also acutely aware of our limited understanding of the various realities of the region's situation and the limits of our potential to provide some solution. These were not merely an intellectual or philosophical recognition of our limitations but an honest self-assessment of our knowledge and capacities.

Let me give you a personal example. Early on, I embarked on what I believed would be a promising economic venture: cultivating cassava and bananas on a one-hectare plot of land. This initial leap into agricultural production offered me priceless insights into the nuances of farming and livestock management, considering the countless technological limitations and environmental factors of the Norte del Cauca region. It shed light on the significant hurdles local farmers encounter across the production cycle. However, rather than a heroic success, this attempt ended in failure.

Through this experience, I recognized my limits and acquired a profound respect and admiration for the knowledge farmers in Norte del Cauca possessed. How did they achieve success when others like myself failed? What ancestral knowledge and capacity do they possess about nature that enables them to make thoughtful day-to-day decisions? The farmers consistently confront critical decisions to secure their daily livelihoods. They make choices such as determining what to plant at a given time, establishing the optimal planting schedule based on historical rainfall patterns, especially in the absence of irrigation, selecting the most suitable seeds, efficiently managing labor allocation, and executing planting and other cultural practices within stringent timelines. These factors ultimately converge within the variable and uncertain landscape of marketing agricultural produce, often under unfavorable circumstances. The farmers in Norte del Cauca were not backward. They were brilliant. And they had much more to teach me regarding farming and many other things. So what did I have to offer them? Who was I to diagnose their problems? Did I have some solution to share?

At the heart of our approach, which we came to in Norte del Cauca, the cornerstone was a constant dialogue of knowledges, an essential element for bridging differences and jointly constructing something of great significance. We resolved to distance ourselves from the conventional paradigm prevalent in many agricultural extension programs, where there may be prejudice toward the farmers and where an "expert" imparts knowledge to them, passive recipients. Simultaneously, as mentioned earlier, our approach recognized that all could contribute to knowledge in their own way based on their language, background, and experience. We did not idealize equality as some romantic notion. We were equal but were not all the same. Instead, we sought to create an approach founded on the principles of embracing and valuing diversity while upholding the knowledge and experiences of each participant. It was a true partnership, driven by a collective mission to enhance alternative production systems by blending/combining/integrating/uniting modern science with the rich wisdom of the farmer. This dynamic gave rise to fresh insights born from the dialogue of knowledges.

Bradley

Haleh, building relationships of trust, which you discussed first, is both the end and necessary means for establishing what Gustavo has called a dialogue of knowledges. The end and the means are quite linked together. It may seem quite simple in theory, but trust and dialogue may be some of the most critical steps missed in many development initiatives worldwide due to the diagnostic or interventionist framing of projects. There is less appreciation for understanding the history of a people and a place. In perhaps worst cases, there can be a false dialogue or an instrumentalization of a dialogue through which outside experts direct the conversation, define the problem, or coordinate the endeavor with some input. Gustavo, can you share some examples of how you developed these relationships of trust and dialogue?

Gustavo

Our relationship with the community deepened through a concerted effort to understand their daily lives. Every person we met offered invaluable insights and wisdom, enriching our understanding. We prioritized building personal connections by consistently visiting different families in the area. These visits were a window into their lives, allowing us to grasp their family dynamics, occupations, land resources, agricultural involvement, and economic circumstances. As familiarity grew, we learned about their aspirations, challenges, and the diverse hurdles they faced. These ongoing interactions knit us closer, fostering a profound and lasting bond with the community.

Our encounter with Sofonias Banguero's family vividly demonstrates the importance of attentive listening and the rewards of mutual learning. While Sofonias primarily dedicated himself to excavating wells rather than farming, Mauricio Lopez, a mechanical engineer from FUNDAEC, took a keen interest in studying and refining Sofonias' established well-digging techniques. The aim was to streamline the process and improve the quality of the extracted water. A refined technique emerged through collaborative efforts and knowledge sharing, jointly developed by both parties. FUNDAEC then extended financial support for the implementation of these improvements. Today, Sofonias still stands as a valuable asset in addressing a pressing need within the community.

Sofonias Banguero testing one of the wells produced by his enterprise

At a particular juncture, Sofonias graciously invited us to observe his operations, an opportunity we eagerly embraced to glean insights into his managerial approach and existing accounting methods. Initially, we believed our input could refine certain aspects of his administration. Our subsequent visit aimed to ensure the solidity of Sofonias' business through robust management and accounting systems. Upon visiting, our anticipation turned to pleasant surprise. Sofonias' daughter, actively engaged in overseeing the accounts, had devised a simple yet astoundingly effective system. This system adeptly tracked orders, managed accounts receivable and payable, and accurately computed the expenses tied to each completed well. It soon became apparent that our contribution to enhancing the efficiency of her system would be minimal. Consequently, this remarkable example transformed into a valuable case study highlighted in our educational materials.

Haleh

When discussing the idea of a dialogue of knowledges, one segment from a speech Farzam gave at the graduation ceremony of FUNDAEC's first student cohort remains etched in my memory. I recently returned to the extracted text from his talk in a magazine we published in the 1980s. On that occasion, he spoke of one of his early explorations into understanding the lives of the local community, which began with his interactions with Julia Vasquez, a remarkable elderly woman who lived to be 90 years old.

Farzam recalled how he would frequently sit on Doña Julia's La Dominga patio, with her gazing out towards the farm ahead, occasionally uttering a few words or observing her great-grandchildren at play in the courtyard. "Now," he reflects, "I realize that during these moments, I was learning from her to look at the world from a very different perspective, through the eyes of a farmer." He then goes on to say that he had always believed that despite the numerous implications of propaganda and racial and class prejudice, being a farmer should be a source of pride.

In his view, a truly just society should place a significantly higher value on its farmers, the individuals who produce its most essential commodity: food. "The conversations with Doña Julia confirmed me even more in this position," he says, "and at the same time taught me a multitude of things that I did not know. Seen through her perspective, the world appeared not as the destitute, embittered, and despondent realm often perceived by intellectuals. While there existed suffering and material impoverishment, days without sustenance and an extraordinary battle for survival, there also thrived faith and hope, kindness and courtesy, and an integrity that seems to be rapidly diminishing in so-called developed societies."

What I find particularly fascinating about Farzam's recollection is that, through clear language and by narrating his initial meetings with Doña Julia, he reveals the genesis of the ideas contained in the book *Rural University*[21] in his mind:

> I realized that, contrary to the prevailing illiteracy rates and the common discourse on the country's educational challenges, Doña Julia had much wisdom to offer the rest of the world. She held knowledge that could benefit others greatly if only they took the time to listen. However, she also recognized that she could benefit from modern science, understanding that it held valuable knowledge to enhance the quality of life for both herself and her great-grandchildren. As our discussions progressed with my fellow colleagues in the establishment of FUNDAEC, the idea of the Rural University emerged strongly. It was envisioned as a place where modern science would interact with the rich wisdom represented by Doña Julia, fostering the creation of new alternatives and the design of improved paths for development. Doña Julia, being of advanced age, had limited interaction with FUNDAEC, and her great-grandchildren were very young. It now falls upon you…to commence this learning journey in the Norte del Cauca region.

Bradley

Hearing these words is beautiful; they remind me of my first impressions of FUNDAEC. In one of my earliest efforts to study the experience in Colombia, I read the book *Rural University: Learning about Education and Development*[22] by Farzam, which followed the first decade of FUNDAEC's work in the region. It documented the period from 1974 to 1982. This period would have been when many of these ideas about the dialogue of knowledges became clear. That book was the first time I had heard of the early participants in FUNDAEC's programs in the region. In particular, I think it was the first time I read about the Ingenieros—the youth who had first responded to the call of FUNDAEC. I was struck reading that book as an undergraduate student in the late 1990s by the honorable ways Farzam had described the people of the region and how the Ingenieros were represented in that text as bringing diverse knowledge and experiences and were equals in the work. There was no hint of superiority in the text. You could tell how much the Ingenieros inspired the thinking and development of FUNDAEC as an institution.

---

[21] Arbab, F. (1984). *Rural university: learning about education and development.* Ottawa: IDRC.

[22] Ibid.

Farzam Arbab in class with the Ingenieros, 1980s

Gustavo

Yes, our experience with the Ingenieros left a lasting impression on us. Through these early collaborators, we got to know many different aspects of the region of Norte del Cauca. For example, I remember that one Ingeniero was a traditional and small-scale farmer working with his family and his parents. But another was a tailor; he used to make pants and shirts. He lived on a farm but did not dedicate himself to farming. There was another who was more committed to activism; he was more an activist than a farmer or an agriculturalist. It was a combination of people with different levels of formal education, too. Some had only finished the first or the first five years of primary education, and others had completed some years of secondary education. Their education was very diverse. However, in the final analysis, they were all the same in relation to the studies they did with us, even though each may come at questions from a distinct perspective.

The Ingenieros were like a mirror of the region and a mirror of the various situations in the region. For example, through Maricela Viveros, we learned to truly recognize the importance of the role of the extended family in the lives of individuals and communities. We knew her grandmother and her mother and the kinds of relationships that she had with her extended family and kinship network. With this example and the family of Maricela and others like her future husband Alfaro Mina, we learned the importance of the extended family relationships that create bonds among many people in the region. We also learned from the Ingenieros that most young girls' best option was to go to Cali to work as maids. They knew about that reality because it was the experience in their extended family network. As members of extended farming families, they were quite familiar with the realities of the changes in the land, the loss of their ancestral land, how sugarcane had come, the impact of chemical insecticides, the decline of water access due to its diversion to a large-scale farmer, and a range of health problems in the community. By working with the Ingenieros and their extended families, we became closer to all the problems confronted in people's lives. We owe them and their families all that first deeper connection with the region.

Through the Ingenieros and their extended family, we could also explore other dimensions of the reality of the people of Norte del Cauca. We learned about their values, beliefs, and cultural, social, and religious practices, and we could perceive the depth of their spiritual understanding and appreciate their intimate connection with Divinity. Because of this belief in God and their sense of spirituality, they held in high esteem the rectitude of conduct and the qualities that emanate from the spirit. They had identified the need to oppose the overwhelming forces of materialism consciously. They sought to preserve their inherited values, which had knitted together the social fabric of their communities: friendship, compassion, solidarity, cooperation, and mutual aid. They also sought to find their true identity, struggled to preserve unity and keep hope alive—the hope that enabled them to exist amidst such hardship.

This feeling we sensed among the people in the communities aligned with our conviction that no matter how advanced the scientific and technological proposals in the field of development may be, they cannot neglect what we can learn from religion, its laws, its spiritual values, and its relevance in the search for solutions to problems and their causes. It was clear to us that any proposal that sought the advancement of a people was incomplete if it ignored or relegated religion and spirituality to a secondary plane. This affinity of beliefs with the population of Norte del Cauca led to more open dialogue and a deeper and more comprehensive exploration of the forces that contribute to or hinder progress toward enhancing community well-being.

Perhaps because we embraced this open dialogue in search of knowledge contained in science and religion, our conversations may have been misinterpreted as indoctrination by some external observers. However, a development strategy whose center is access to knowledge could not surrender the value of spirituality and morality held so centrally to people's lives, nor could it exclude the analysis of spiritual reality simply because of an outdated concept of religion. We have always wondered if the work of FUNDAEC would have gone further in the past 50 years had it not been for the obstacles created along the way by the ever-present religious prejudice we encountered.

Bradley

When FUNDAEC set out on this path in the 1970s, many movements and development initiatives were making massive promises: promises of national liberation and revolution, agricultural modernization, or an era of high consumption. Many of these drew millions and millions of young people into their ranks. We have seen how these movements did not realize many of their goals, and many people worldwide have grown weary of promises unkept or may even be cynical about the possibility of bringing about a better world. I do not mean to make light of the incredible hope associated with a yearning for change in these movements over the past 50 years. Having engaged with and studied them closely, the ideals they are associated with inspire me, too. I simply mean that individuals and institutions tied to raising those hopes and possibilities have also sometimes built that hope on weak premises that failed to deliver, and reshaped lives in ways that left people and communities in even worse conditions than before, no matter the ideal envisioned. So, by bringing this into the conversation, I want to note that this is no light matter; it is heavy.

The dialogues in Norte del Cauca were very different from most development projects or movements one could encounter at the time, although they were no doubt running in parallel. So, the relationship you struck with the Ingenieros and their families seemed to deviate from many approaches at that time. How did working with the Ingenieros and their extended families enable FUNDAEC to take its first steps in developing its distinctive approach to development practice?

Haleh

In the 1970s, the prevailing discourse on development and other movements centered itself around the crucial concept of participation; it suggested that the success of projects and campaigns depended on the degree and depth of local community involvement and that the absence of such participation was a significant factor contributing to failures. At the time, there were extensive discussions regarding the multifaceted nature of community participation in development. For instance, in extension programs—whether focused on agriculture, health, or other domains aimed at imparting specific knowledge to local populations—participation often took the form of soliciting people's feedback and involvement in designing and implementing the programs.

The discourse recognized that for community participation to increase, individuals from rural backgrounds needed to be empowered to serve as catalysts for positive change across various domains to improve the quality of life in their local communities. Consequently, numerous individuals and groups established programs to train literacy educators, health promoters, and agricultural extension workers. These initiatives often required individuals to enroll in schools far from their hometowns, where they underwent comprehensive training in diverse fields. Subsequently, they returned to their home communities with technical knowledge, technological insights, and practical expertise.

These individuals, frequently drawn from the younger generation, played a pivotal role by providing development organizations and practitioners with invaluable insights into the communities they served. Nonetheless, these initiatives faced a significant challenge: developing training programs that equipped youth with the necessary skills and knowledge to engage with their communities effectively. Additionally, a formidable task was to instill in them the desire and determination to remain in their communities and become agents of positive change. Many were lured away from their community by job opportunities or sought further education in different regions of the country, making retention of youth and creative people in the community a pressing concern.

But FUNDAEC's experience, rooted in its approach, was different; the youth became even more committed to their communities, hopeful, not despairing, and did not become alienated from the region. They stayed. There was great care in elevating the dignity of the youth and acknowledging the great value of their identity and heritage. FUNDAEC sought to fortify and elevate their love for their Afro-Colombian roots and to appreciate the resilience of their communities in the face of historic oppression. Rather than drawing them away from their identities, lives, families, and communities, the educational process served them in their homeplaces and collective search for alternative, more viable development paths.

FUNDAEC did not bring the Ingenieros away from their villages to a central place to train to be agents of change. There was no indoctrination, as Gustavo noted before. FUNDAEC worked with them in the communities to develop their scientific capacity, gather knowledge and observations, describe their social and environmental context, and systematically analyze, consult, and communicate results. FUNDAEC almost immediately invited them to join action-research teams to deepen their collective understanding of the region, the communities, and the families in their villages and surrounding areas.

Ingenieros working together on an agricultural project

First group of Ingenieros gathered at FUNDAEC's facility in La Arrobleda, 1980s

But, at the same time, this learning process did not deny them the value of their existing knowledge, which their extended families transferred to them through generations, ancestral knowledge that enabled them to interpret their realities and provided a resource of hope. But FUNDAEC also did not shy away from important spiritual themes in people's lives. There were extended periods of consultation on the importance of moral values such as honesty, sincerity, truthfulness, and service to others that built bonds between us and reinforced the focus on a commitment to the people, their extended families, and the region over the long-term.

Bradley

What I hear emerging in this period and place is a dialogue of knowledges leading to new insights and trust but also a different kind of mutual commitment from FUNDAEC and between the Ingenieros and their extended families. The commitments were cascading. We often think of commitment as something one does as an individual or institution. One forms a commitment. We say, as individuals, that we are committed to carrying out some actions or we are committed to some people. But what I see in FUNDAEC and its experience in Norte del Cauca differs greatly. It did not make commitments in isolation. You both describe a sense of collective or mutual commitment forged—knitting together of commitments. These early experiences with the Ingenieros fostered a recognition that when one makes a genuine effort—as an individual or institution—it also attracts the goodwill, solidarity, effort, and unity of wider collectivities—of entire communities—in particular places and regions. It builds a social fabric. The region of Norte del Cauca and the pressing challenges people were confronting catalyzed that sense of mutual commitment. There was more than just a dialogue of knowledges at work but also a mutual commitment to action that demanded more from everyone involved. In other words, the dialogue of knowledges evolved into a relationship of mutual commitment, the knitting together of a fabric of solidarity.

It is hard to believe that so much of FUNDAEC's vision emerged in these early years and all of the learning that was taking place in Norte del Cauca in those days. In one way, when I listen to what you both are sharing, I think to myself, this is all very complex. And, of course, on the other hand, it is all very simple. Maybe another way to put it is that FUNDAEC began as a rather modest attempt to build meaningful relationships that grew in complexity over time. One of the principles of FUNDAEC's work that I frequently share with my collaborators and students is beginning with modest initiatives. One of FUNDAEC's documents reads: "Experience has shown that development processes must begin with modest initiatives."[23] I often refer back to this as a check on my actions. In many cases in development, there are big promises made about certain interventions, and people feel the commitment is too much or you lose people's trust.

But FUNDAEC did not approach things this way. It began, as Gustavo described, by visiting the homes of families and connecting with youth who wanted to participate in serving their community. It's interesting because when you begin with modest goals and you achieve

[23] Karlberg, M. and Correa, B. (2016) 'Development as systematic learning and capacity building', in Skinner, A., Smith M.B., Brown, E. and Troll, T. *Education, learning and the transformation of development.* New York: Routledge, pp. 19-35.

them, you develop faith with people that you can achieve something more significant. It may begin with meeting a few people, and then, over time, confidence builds. In many development projects, we might set the expectations of finding and implementing solutions so high that people can lose faith in their ability to change a situation because the goal is so large, the timeline too long, and the expectations unreasonable or overly ambitious. We see this in many movements—people losing faith or hope in progress either from fear of failure, lack of confidence, or disbelief that change can happen due to broken promises.

Again, this concept of modesty may be worth exploring further here when considering the dialogue of knowledges and how FUNDAEC began its work in Norte del Cauca. Modesty connects back to being honest about what one can do and not over-promising and under-delivering. It is a caution against cheapening a given process by saying, "Oh, we can get here quickly. Just cut some corners, and we'll get there," or alternately making some big promise that one has no way of achieving and people don't believe in. Why begin with modest initiatives? What is it about beginning with modest initiatives that were crucial to FUNDAEC's work?

Haleh

You have brought up an interesting point, Bradley. You have discussed shared commitment and perceptively highlighted modesty as a defining characteristic of FUNDAEC's work. When reflecting on modesty, I can't help but draw a contrast with arrogance. Arrogance often stems from a sense of self-importance and superiority. It becomes evident when an individual or a group believes they can attain excessive power and control over the world. Arrogance blinds people to the complexities of the human condition and makes them insensitive to the interconnections in our world. It distorts one's perception of reality, often leading one to set unattainable goals and even make promises that one cannot fulfill.

However, we frequently misunderstand modesty. And, at times, arrogance disguises itself as modesty, with individuals pretending to be disinterested or ignorant. This type of false modesty can be even more problematic than blatant arrogance. A genuinely modest person can have ambitious aspirations, striving for substantial and fundamental changes because they recognize the world's pressing needs. They take proactive steps, deeply reflect, and maintain a firm connection to reality. They understand the limits of achievable change but don't limit their vision to short-term goals. They possess a clear, long-term vision but approach it with deliberate, gradual steps, learning from their experiences. They know that meaningful change takes time, commitment, and hard work. In this sense, they are realistic.

Despite the prevalent misperception of science, it embodies a form of modesty. Science pursues lofty objectives but does so through gradual, incremental steps. Authentic scientists comprehend the enormity of creation and have a great deal of humility. They acknowledge their smallness in comparison to the vastness of the universe. When we contemplate FUNDAEC's experience, it becomes evident that it embodies a modesty akin to that of a true scientist. From the beginning, even as FUNDAEC aimed to effect profound and lasting change, it conscientiously focused on a limited number of students, immersing itself in the region's reality and earnestly striving to understand the needs and challenges of the local population.

Importantly, impulsive activism or a trial-and-error mentality did not drive FUNDAEC's early efforts. The founders did not adopt a "let's do this and see what happens" approach, nor did they exhibit curiosity to observe how people would respond or set up experiments to measure the effects of their interventions on their students or the local populace. The term "experimentation" was avoided because it implied a willingness to treat people's lives as variables. Instead, they took modest steps alongside the community, assessing the risks of each decision and considering the potential impact on people's lives. This approach sharply contrasts with overconfidence, where individuals claim to possess all the answers, seek personal acclaim, and strive to etch their names into the annals of history.

However, modesty should not be confused with complacency or a lack of ambition. A modest individual can set ambitious goals and strive to achieve significant accomplishments. Humility does not hinder aspiration; instead, it can coexist with a strong drive to accomplish great things, demonstrating that modesty and aspiration are not mutually exclusive but can complement each other in the journey toward meaningful success. This discussion reminds me of another part of the speech that Farzam gave at the graduation of the Ingenieros. He talked about working diligently within one's limits while simultaneously acknowledging the intricacies and magnitude of the overarching issues. In that address, he articulated his paramount concern for the well-being of the people in the region—a concern deeply shared by FUNDAEC and its collaborators, including the Ingenieros themselves.

> ... one question continues to worry me: what about the well-being of the inhabitants of this region? When will we really see the results of your work and that of the technicians and promoters who follow you? I am sure that many of my friends would tell me that I should not be so ambitious, that humanity's problems are big and that a small group should not expect spectacular results and should be content with small contributions. After all, there are

more than two billion people in the world living in extreme poverty, of which 800 million are said to be continually living under conditions of hunger. Clearly I have to accept this point of view with humility. We should not demand large solutions from a small group of people and a relatively small effort like FUNDAEC. But the question remains, where should we look for great solutions to humanity's problems?

First graduation ceremony of Ingenieros and Promoters of Community Well-being, La Arrobleda, 1980s

Interwoven Commitments

*I ponder whether we can achieve anything significant in this
world without the efforts of those willing to relinquish things
dear to them in a given moment for something of greater value,
particularly when it has profound implications for the lives of others.*

Haleh Arbab

Opening

In the first conversation, we discussed how, in the early years of the formation of FUNDAEC, its founders established meaningful relationships in the region through principled actions that opened up the possibility for long-term development processes rooted in educational programming. FUNDAEC forged these relationships in constant dialogue with the people of the region. Distinct attitudes guided this dialogue, attitudes that opened pathways to collaboration and fostered initiative, mutual commitment, and dedication to specific lines of action determined by the groups involved, particularly in participatory action-research efforts to promote small-scale agriculture and broader rural development initiatives in Norte del Cauca.

The profound learning in the first decade in the formative years of FUNDAEC catalyzed through the work in the region of Norte del Cauca raised a new generation of Promoters of Community Well-being in those communities—the Ingenieros. These early experiences yielded new insights into the emerging formulation of an approach to education for development that would serve other Colombian communities and regions and, in later decades, extend its scope to other countries. The precious experience in Norte del Cauca, the gems of wisdom from the dialogue between knowledge and action in that region, would also be carried forward, shaping the principles of the organization at an almost molecular level in every growth phase.

This chapter focuses on how the interweaving of commitments beyond Norte del Cauca propelled a process of organic growth. The organic growth of FUNDAEC from its formative years in Norte del Cauca to reach other regions of Colombia, forge new partnerships with collaborators, systematize education materials, and raise an even greater number of Promoters of Community Well-being is a crucial part of this story. Yet, the experience of FUNDAEC's expansion beyond Norte del Cauca is not germane to this institutional experience alone. Another concern in education and development is scaling up and the appropriateness of replicating, transferring, extending, or propagating an approach created in one place or region with its specific goals, logics, and conditions of possibility to another. The appropriateness of scaling methods is an especially important concern to development practitioners who are careful not to impose the values, models, and technologies created in one place upon people who some believe are lacking or in need of those things in another. Indeed, the annals of development thought and practice are replete with such arrogant tendencies and historical accounts in which a rather narrow conception of development—for instance, the application of agro-industrial technologies—is imposed upon communities while disregarding their knowledge or valuing their aspirations are all too common.

In this next conversation, we will focus on how FUNDAEC scaled its initiatives. As we find in the previous dialogue, where the impulse and intention to serve and build mutually committed relationships exist, expanding the reach of those relationships, bonds, and activities to more people emerges organically and reciprocally. As more people become involved, more people may wish to become involved. Moreover, as capacity develops within an institution to serve more people and initiatives, questions emerge about its responsibility to grow. Therefore, in the words of development practitioners, institutions often come to a moment in which they must decide how to scale up the initiatives undertaken to reach more people in ways that do not distort the principled intent. The question of appropriate scale—how many people, communities, and regions—became a crucial point of consultation among those participating in FUNDAEC's early work.

Bradley

Given the depth of the experience in Norte del Cauca described in the previous conversation, how did FUNDAEC decide to extend its reach into collaborations in other places in Colombia? What opportunities and concerns guided those considerations?

Gustavo

A strong bond had been forged with the people of Norte del Cauca, steadily becoming a secure foundation for future endeavors; FUNDAEC established mutual trust, open communication, and acceptance; there was widespread recognition by the community of the progress so far achieved; it had established a well-conceived program for the education of their youth; acceptance of the alternative agricultural and livestock production systems developed was growing; a credit fund for innovative financing for small productive projects was operating, and burgeoning structures of community organization were emerging. FUNDAEC proved the efficacy of its educational content and pedagogy in instilling a sense of service, sensitivity, and commitment to the community among groups of young people, empowering them with the skills for research and the design and execution of collective initiatives. The experience validated our assertion of the indispensability of an educational institution in a region dedicated to generating knowledge for advancing a specific population.

At this juncture, we had to decide where to direct our efforts as we ventured into the next phase. Ongoing conversations with other like-minded organizations, within and outside the region, familiar with FUNDAEC's work significantly influenced the path forward. Among them were entities promoting producer associations, others designing credit systems for specific rural populations, some creating or adapting appropriate technologies, and others promoting small rural enterprises or supporting community organizations. Simultaneously, some were more politically driven and committed to championing the social and cultural aspirations of the local people. Reflecting on the process and outcome of the training of the first FUNDAEC graduates, we all agreed that the impact of the programs they were engaged in would significantly benefit from introducing a similar educational component. They needed collaborators with a more integrated vision of development as well as more exposure to knowledge beyond their own area of expertise, and opportunities to refine skills and attitudes suitable for community work. So, why not consider that the content developed by FUNDAEC with the Ingenieros could serve this purpose?

Haleh

Through its work with the Ingenieros and their families, FUNDAEC confirmed the importance of having appropriate institutions for generating, applying, and disseminating knowledge. It saw a well-structured educational process as a crucial element for the meaningful participation of young people and as a prerequisite for an authentic and sustainable development process in a region.

When establishing its initial educational program with the Ingenieros, FUNDAEC argued that a region's ability to participate in a learning and decision-making process for its development hinged on having a population capable of comprehensively analyzing regional issues and opportunities while seeking viable solutions. However, recognizing that existing educational institutions in the region were not adequately preparing people with these skills, FUNDAEC prioritized the creation of an institution for the generation and application of knowledge and a program to train a new breed of professionals capable of collaborating with rural families to address a range of issues, including health, nutrition, housing, agricultural production, income, and community organization, all from within the community itself. The Ingenieros were the first graduates of this program and its earliest champions.

From left to right, Alberto Alzate, Rosa Orejuela, Francia Valcárcel, and unidentified at graduation of Ingenieros, La Arrobleda, 1983

During these years, FUNDAEC dedicated its efforts to establishing a new kind of learning institution in the heart of the region. This approach, however, differed from traditional schools or universities, as it aimed to provide the necessary impetus for regional progress by actively serving the rural population where they were—in their hometowns.

FUNDAEC aimed to build educational programs and support action research activities intertwined with specific projects and goals to serve the community. It wanted a curriculum that cultivated the know-how required for young people like the Ingenieros to lead the development processes in their communities and educational materials and experiences that would provide the means for implementing initiatives to enhance the quality of life in the surrounding communities.

Gustavo

The path before us was not necessarily to replicate the experience of the Ingenieros in Norte del Cauca in other places but to create new ways to better put to use what we had achieved. Naturally, we were aware that given what we had learned, we had to stay within the conceptual framework that we clarified and expanded over time through continuous action-reflection: our integrated conception of development as a process in which the community and the individuals that compose it are the main protagonists; our strong belief in the nobility and the latent potential in every human being; the firm commitment to education as the means to awaken the potentialities of the individual to bear abundant fruits for the benefit of the individual and society; our belief in the indispensability of access to knowledge for all protagonists; and the centrality of generating knowledge based on what is learned from science, religion, and experience.

The fruit of all these reflections and deliberations was the creation of an educational system that allowed easy access and adaptation to the diverse conditions of rural regions in Colombia. The learning from the practices of the Ingenieros, who were prepared through the first texts of the FUNDAEC curriculum to form groups of young people and adults in their communities, led to the concept of tutorial learning. The Ingenieros would form small groups in different communities to study these initial educational texts, which aimed at developing scientific, mathematical, technological, and language skills. Thus, different components came together to create what would henceforth be called the Sistema de Aprendizaje Tutorial (SAT), or Tutorial Learning System.

Haleh

I remember these groups formed by the Ingenieros. Upon my arrival in Colombia, I had the opportunity to observe closely the work of two of the Ingenieros, a husband and wife, in the village of Alegrías. While tending to their family's land, they initiated a collaboration with fellow farmers in the village, engaging in the shared exploration of optimal agricultural practices and strategies to market their produce without succumbing to unjust intermediary fees. During this period, they began preliminary discussions about establishing a village store. The envisioned store aimed to procure local products while offering the community access to a diverse range of goods at more affordable prices. Concurrently, they established a study group comprising young individuals from the village, collectively delving into subjects they had personally explored in their studies and undertaking different projects that would contribute to the betterment of various aspects of the lives of the inhabitants of these communities. Others were doing similar things in their communities. By the time they graduated from their studies, which we described before, almost all had formed study and action groups in their communities. Some of their students were designated Promoters of Community Well-being and graduated alongside the Ingenieros at the first graduation ceremony.

Ingeniero Alfaro Mina with others in Alegrías, 1980s

Early SAT groups tutored by Ingenieros, 1980s

Gustavo

The early success with the Ingenieros gave us confidence that the SAT (el sistema de aprendizaje tutorial) needed to have the ability to reproduce itself by acquiring the characteristics of organic growth. The seed for propagation became a group of 10–15 people, a sequence of texts in the areas mentioned above, and a tutor to guide the study of the texts and corresponding practices. The fertile ground was the rural communities that understood the scope of the educational process and identified a local person to be trained as a tutor. The collaborating institution responsible for the program in a region would appoint a coordinator and connect them to the group. Regular orientation visits of the coordinators to the groups would act as the revitalizing rain that fostered the growth and development of the seed.

With the SAT, FUNDAEC found a sustainable expansion scheme for a rural educational program, building centers of learning in other regions and promoting development strategies within its conceptual framework. Identifying an already established institution with commitment and effective leadership was the starting point for forming a nucleus of new centers of learning in a particular region. Their task, now added to their usual activities, was strengthening the ongoing educational processes with the population they served.

From another perspective, the SAT introduced a novel rural education program that broke with the widespread perception of education in rural areas as contextless, of low quality, difficult to access, especially for women, and with high levels of school dropout. In this way, the SAT program was consolidated, quickly becoming a promising alternative for rural education in Colombia, with around 40 institutions, 20,000 students, and 270 municipalities.

Bradley

How did this transition to developing an educational program that you could replicate in other regions affect your relationships with the Ingenieros? What was their role moving forward?

Haleh

The graduation of the Ingenieros marked the culmination of this successful experience and a period of intense learning. The dilemma was whether they should collaborate with other organizations and in other locations or remain dedicated to continuing the work in Norte del Cauca. The latter seemed challenging due to financial constraints and resource involvement. Despite this, the Ingenieros were highly capable individuals, contributing significantly to advancing processes in Norte del Cauca.

Yet the question remained. How would the Ingenieros continue contributing to FUNDAEC's ongoing work and the growth of new learning centers? Would they merely graduate and move on? External observers who interacted with the Ingenieros recognized their great capacity. I remember Farzam speaking once about this dilemma when an international visitor with experience in rural development asked one of the Ingenieros what they would do when they left the program. Speaking to the Ingenieros and referencing one of them, Alirio Sanchez, who had addressed the visitor, Farzam said:

> I think it was Alirio that said that this idea of entering and leaving had no meaning, no sense to you. He was referring to the fact that within the philosophical conception of FUNDAEC, the idea of the school as a space within four walls, separated from the community, the family and real life did not exist. No one has entered The Rural University and no one will leave it. An institution was created that belonged to all the inhabitants of this region, an institution that would investigate problems of different kinds, in agriculture, in health and sanitation, in education, in the marketing system, in access to information and in community organization, an institution where we would all learn together and all work for the common purpose of achieving greater degrees of well-being.

The idea that one does not enter or leave The Rural University raises the question of how such a center of learning would sustain its mission in a region. In other words, how would the participants, such as the Ingenieros from the community, propagate the approach by reaching out to and involving others in the region to participate, let alone operate beyond the bounds of the region? As Gustavo has said, the seedbed for sustaining and growing the reach of the rural university even in the 1970s had become a group of 10–15 people, a sequence of texts, and a tutor (who at that time would be one of the Ingenieros), to guide the study of the texts and corresponding practices. Yet questions remained about how this would continue.

With the Ingenieros' work in their villages, it was time to address the question of human resources within every locality. Who were the catalysts of change in each community, and what capabilities did they need to develop to fulfill this role? Thus, emerged the idea of a pyramid of workers for community well-being, fostering the engagement of a diverse group of young individuals at various levels. At the foundational level of this pyramid were the Promoters of Community Well-being. These individuals, having undergone specific training through FUNDAEC's texts focusing on developing mathematical, scientific, language and communication, technological, and community service skills, were equipped to initiate modest health, agriculture, and literacy initiatives within their communities.

Participants undertaking an experiment, La Arrobleda, 1980s

Moving up the pyramid, the technician and the high school equivalent comprised the subsequent levels. These individuals underwent more advanced training, preparing them to undertake more intricate acts of service in their respective communities. The community could leverage a spectrum of talents and capabilities through this structure, ensuring a comprehensive approach to addressing their unique needs and challenges.

In this way, the sistema de aprendizaje tutorial unfolded as FUNDAEC created the instructional materials. However, in preparing and teaching the materials, a crucial consideration arose regarding who would teach these materials. The tutoring process demanded a holistic understanding of integrated knowledge, transcending the traditional compartmentalization of subjects like mathematics, science, and technology. While the Ingenieros had initiated tutoring in small groups within their villages, FUNDAEC recognized the imperative of training additional tutors, thus emerging the need for a systematic approach to tutor training.

Furthermore, recognizing the need for institutional support, it became apparent that an entity must underpin this process. This realization led to the identification of three fundamental components: an institution, a tutor, and a group of students. During office discussions, the insight emerged that this system was replicable. The foundational elements—the tutor, the group, and the textbooks—constituted the essence of the SAT program. This seed was the key for replication, adaptable to the diverse requirements of different institutions. Consequently, the Sistema de Aprendizaje Tutorial took a concrete form, embodying the principles of a comprehensive and replicable approach to education.

Bradley

Gustavo and Haleh, what you have described—the culmination of a decade of action research, the engagement with the Ingenieros, the promoters, the emergence of a rural educational approach built on a sistema de aprendizaje tutorial—departed from so many of the established conventions in education and development, particularly those promoted by traditional universities. From the vantage point of a scholar at a land grant university in the United States, I have seen firsthand how certain conventions in program development, technology transfer, and community outreach and education have reproduced damaging dynamics in communities. Both in West Virginia and Nicaragua, I have witnessed these approaches.

Conventions in education, research, and outreach are still very firmly held in land grant universities in the United States; that science, education, and development practice is something that a particular group of professionals does; that the designs of development are established and experimented within a particular university institution where they generate knowledge and technologies to be then transferred outward into communities who receive these benefits from the outside in. In the parlance of US land grant universities, this is the basic model for extension.

In many ways, we still see a dominant model of extension where a consultant, an extension agent, or a nonprofit organization–educated outside of the community runs a program or workshops–offers some short-term educational outreach, or provides technical assistance on a very narrow subject matter or technical fix that may or may not be of particular concern or interest to the community at large. Yet, this model of developing technical packages, programs, or solutions in traditional universities and delivering them in communities was undoubtedly not the approach practiced by FUNDAEC nor conceptualized in its vision for centers of learning. So, what strikes me is how differently FUNDAEC was thinking about extension.

I can only imagine in the 1970s–1980s, when considering how you might begin to expand the approach to other regions of Colombia—as others began to see the opportunities to collaborate with FUNDAEC— that you would be concerned with the way it would evolve or might deviate from its principled actions as it was being adapted to new regions and utilized by others. I am sure you were worried about how this experience in Norte del Cauca might travel elsewhere and reach other communities. In other words, it raised a question of how the model would scale up or extend beyond the initial region. What was the nature of the process through which an experience focused on a specific region and under very particular conditions became a viable alternative for rural education for diverse populations in Colombia?

Gustavo

I can confidently say that this was not a premeditated process, nor did it follow a macro plan to scale up a successful experience. It was a true organic process that developed and adapted to multiple specific circumstances. Early on, we realized it wasn't simply about expanding coverage or replicating a successful program. While the program's growth hinted at an expansive future, it also involved the transferring and adapting an educational model designed to empower a specific population.

The increase in numbers wasn't our primary concern in the growth process; other fundamental questions needed attention: What would be the nature of the expected change in the institutions adopting the program, the participating students, the community's perception, and the funding organizations supporting the program? How could we ensure that, over time, those involved were internalizing the ideas, methods, and strategies? These and other questions and their respective answers defined our approach and activities in managing the program's expansion over several years.

I remember with great satisfaction when Francisco Alzate, an enthusiast of rural education from Apía (one of the municipalities in the department of Risaralda), visited our offices in Cali. Accompanied by two municipal officials, their mission was to request our collaboration in making middle and high school education more accessible to young men and women who, for various reasons, couldn't travel from their places of residence to the municipal center. They had heard about FUNDAEC's experience in Norte del Cauca and, after reviewing some of the SAT educational materials, were convinced of how applicable this innovation was for their region. At this first meeting, we agreed to make an exploratory visit to Risaralda to better understand its reality and the other key players involved.

After our visit to Apía and its surroundings to better understand its reality and protagonists, and after several conversations, we agreed to formalize our collaboration by signing an agreement. In this agreement, FUNDAEC committed to advising the Municipality's Education Secretary officials in selecting the initial tutors, providing training seminars for them, supporting the promotion of the program in the selected rural areas, forming groups, and initiating classes. In turn, the municipality committed to providing the facilities for tutor training, remunerating them, and offering all the necessary institutional support for the program's operation.

The path to the full operation of the program turned out to be one filled with many obstacles, as we faced situations very different from what we expected. It was not easy to explain and help the first students and their parents understand an educational program that challenged traditional concepts of schooling. It was like going against the conventional idea of school as a fixed physical space with established schedules, following an official curriculum, and featuring a teacher who delivers lessons. Only after much dialogue and as students advanced in their studies and experienced transformations in their lives did they begin to dispel their doubts about the tutorial methodology, the usefulness of the content, and its applicability in daily life.

Francisco Alzate, enthusiastic and dedicated promoter of SAT in the department of Risaralda

Despite some attrition, as is to be expected when implementing an unfamiliar educational experience, the students who persevered became the program's strongest advocates. Over time and through many conversations, they learned the vocabulary and narrative to explain the innovative initiative in which they participated. It was an educational program that referred to teachers as "tutors," transformed classrooms into SAT groups that met in flexible locations, and had students dedicate an average of only 15 hours per week to group study at flexible schedules. Practices were carried out directly in the community. Instead of a fragmented list of courses, the program prioritized the theoretical and practical study of a sequence of texts aimed at developing the capabilities necessary to become drivers of community wellbeing.

Furthermore, this program adopted a holistic approach that encouraged students to explore and refine their spiritual qualities, develop their character, and gain fundamental scientific knowledge. Through their participation in the educational process, they honed their observation skills, learned to ask meaningful questions, and developed their ability to seek solutions. They also improved their oral and written language abilities and nurtured a genuine drive to serve their community.

With periodic changes in the Secretary of Education, explaining the program's complexities and dispelling doubts and preconceptions became a recurring task. This effort was not always met with the same level of acceptance and commitment. It became evident that these hurdles were intrinsic to institutionalizing a new experience, requiring time and a method refined through experience. Our collaboration with government institutions, as opposed to non-governmental organizations, exacerbated the difficulty as they typically experience more turnover in leadership.

SAT groups from different municipalities of Risaralda gathering to share experiences and celebrate their accomplishments, 1990s

When reflecting on the key factors behind the program's rapid expansion, institutionalization, and permanence in the 14 municipalities of Risaralda, the leadership of Francisco and his group of collaborators stands out. They were widely accepted and respected by various sectors of the community. This experience in Risaralda demonstrated that committed leadership guarantees the success and continuity of the program in a region. The same was evident in other places where the program took root and flourished. Specifically in Risaralda, the presence of an individual like Francisco Alzate—imbued with a genuine educator's spirit, a permanent defender of community initiatives, a selfless and principled political figure, and an unwavering and devoted worker deeply dedicated to rural education—played a determining role in the success of the program. This type of leadership facilitated the seamless integration of the program into the administrative and operational framework of the host institution in all places where it was implemented.

For transferred experiences to have enduring effects, initial actions must involve a robust training component. In our case, this training was not merely about absorbing the content of specific texts and a particular pedagogy but consciously internalizing a vision and conception of development, fostering a resolute commitment to rural education, and allowing moral principles and values to guide actions. The agreements made with participating institutions in the SAT encompassed training sessions at all levels of the institution—directors, program coordinators, and tutor candidates. FUNDAEC also ensured that inter-institutional interactions fostered genuine collaboration and mutual aid and that it reached agreements through consensus and dialogue.

To advance the transfer of the program in Risaralda, we developed a training scheme consisting of seminars lasting one or two weeks, during which tutors discussed theoretical documents, studied SAT texts, reviewed pedagogical concepts, and shared experiences on how to form groups and what complementary activities to use to enhance the study. What we defined in the agreements as 'advisory support' included accompanying visits to the institutions and groups. Interactions with participating institutions primarily took place between the institution's field coordinator and a member of the group in FUNDAEC responsible for coordinating the program at the national level. A constant indicator of the degree of program adoption in each institution was the growth of their institutional capacity to gradually and systematically assume many tasks initially assigned to FUNDAEC.

Bradley

Gustavo and Haleh, I understand that, in addition to strengthening relationships and constant dialogue with various partners across Colombia, FUNDAEC was also deepening its experience with the development and training of tutors. I can imagine that there must have been a great deal of learning about the role and preparation of the program's tutors. Can you elaborate more on how you expanded and replicated the SAT program by recruiting and training tutors?

Gustavo

The process of replicating our educational model in different regions of the country reinforced our initial observation regarding the indispensable role of the tutor in this innovative teaching/learning paradigm. It became increasingly apparent that not only should the training of these tutors be systematic, but it also needed to be continuous. As the program's creators with robust university backgrounds, we initially assumed the role of tutors, followed by the Ingenieros as the second group. However, our formidable challenge arose when we sought capable individuals within the organizations we collaborated with to be trained as tutors.

Initially considering educators already working in rural schools, we soon discovered that many showed little interest in breaking away from conventional schooling. Their mindset was rooted in a curriculum built on isolated courses, hindering knowledge integration and exploration of alternative pedagogies. This experience led us to take another path, turning to young people who had completed secondary school and who, despite lacking formal teacher training, were more receptive to new ideas.

At this juncture, we devised a training scheme centered on discussing the principles of the program, the concept of a rural university, and the study of the content of the texts, emphasizing the importance of practical applications. We also reviewed the curricular elements and the innovative pedagogical approach of the texts. We hold in high esteem the hundreds of tutors who, as pioneers, offered thousands of young people the opportunity to benefit from educational advancements derived from the experience in the Norte del Cauca. These tutors became exemplars of creativity, dedication, sacrifice, a spirit of service, and sensitivity toward others, serving as a perennial source of inspiration for those who followed in their footsteps.

Haleh

Between 1989 and 2009, FUNDAEC provided training to over a thousand individuals from various regions of Colombia as tutors. The need to study more advanced program texts and agreements we made with the Ministry of Education led FUNDAEC to deepen its focus on tutor professionalization during this period. FUNDAEC established a University Center in Norte del Cauca for this training to achieve this. A substantial number of students pursued their studies at the campus of the Centro Universitario de Bienestar Rural, an institution offering a bachelor's degree in rural education, along with two graduate programs—one in education for development and another in the strengthening of local economies, situated in Perico Negro, Cauca. Additionally, other students pursued their educational endeavors in dedicated spaces established in other parts of the country in collaboration with partner organizations that implemented the SAT program.

The curriculum for the bachelor's degree emerged as a tangible outcome of FUNDAEC's extensive research, action, and learning initiatives—all geared towards developing human resources crucial for regional development. Specifically designed to foster educators capable of contributing effectively to societal transformation, the curriculum faced the challenge of seamlessly integrating content, methodologies, and practices. The goal was to equip program participants with diverse capabilities, enabling them to excel as educators whose efforts extend beyond the classroom and encompass many of the diverse life processes in which their students, families, and communities are engaged. This approach treated curriculum design as an ongoing process, where content, methodologies, and practices continually evolved to better achieve educational objectives.

First group of graduates of FUNDAEC's bachelor's degree in rural education, Perico Negro, 1990s

These dedicated individuals, defined by their unwavering commitment to remote regions and their passion for contributing to the education of countless young people, continue to make a positive impact in the different posts where they serve. They are dispersed across diverse locations, from coastal communities like Guapi, Timbiquí, López de Micay, and the port of Buenaventura to the Caribbean shores encompassing the departments of Córdoba, Atlántico, Bolívar, and the Guajira. In addition, many are actively working in educational establishments in the departments of Risaralda, Antioquia, Santander, and Caquetá, further extending the reach of their positive influence on the lives of students, families, and communities.

But, not everyone or every institution saw our work similarly. For instance, I recall a time when there was considerable discussion about rural education. The Ministry of Education supposedly supported the cause, emphasizing the importance of bringing education to

Participants in FUNDAEC's bachelor's degree program in rural education from different regions of Colombia and Latin America

underprivileged communities—a discourse that has resurfaced in public discussions. FUNDAEC emerged not only as a pioneer in rural education through its initial work with Ingenieros and the SAT program but also with the Bachelor's degree program designed to train rural educators. During that period, no program dedicated itself to training teachers for rural areas; we were the first and the only ones in Colombia. And, despite our groundbreaking efforts, we never received financial support. Students made great sacrifices to fund their studies, and the SAT organizations allocated a portion of their budget for tutor training to cover educational expenses. Despite these challenges, we were content, as our focus was on contributing to the cause of rural education, collaborating without expecting anything in return.

Then, one day, the Ministry sent a group of experts from Bogotá. They seemed disoriented and disgruntled, finding fault with having to travel to what they considered a distant and seemingly remote location. The complaint struck us as absurd since the University was only 45 minutes south of Cali. It wasn't the distance that bothered them; it was the rural setting, the farms, the sugarcane, the roads, and even the diversity of people. Upon their arrival, they conducted inspections, offered insults, and, upon returning, documented in their report that this was a university in the "monte."

Edmundo Gutiérrez in class at the University Center
for Rural Well-being, Perico Negro

Today, we are telling the story of a collective endeavor—a tale of a group of individuals united by a dream. They agreed on foundational principles and were convinced of their ability to make that dream a reality. Our conversation offers glimpses into this shared history, revealing the narrative of people who passionately engaged in an endeavor they loved and deeply believed in. This story spans geographical boundaries and generations, providing a mosaic of experiences. While it's impossible to acknowledge everyone who shaped this narrative, that limitation should not deter us from highlighting those who come to mind at various junctures for diverse reasons. For instance, when I think of the bachelor's degree program and all it accomplished, my thoughts naturally gravitate towards my friend and colleague Francia de Valcárcel, an anthropologist heavily committed to FUNDAEC since its early days. Francia accompanied groups of Ingenieros in their studies and interactions with the community. Her keen observational skills and attentive listening were a product of her anthropological training and reflective of her innate human qualities.

One particularly vivid memory from the program's inception involves sitting with Francia and crafting the educational modules for our students. Woven into our texts were exercises and questions designed to prompt reflection on the material and encourage further investigation. Francia placed great importance on these exercises, insisting we avoid rhetorical questions. "What would we respond to this question we just posed? Can we even answer it ourselves?" she would often ask. I learned a valuable lesson during our collaboration—to move away from my position as the writer of the text and get closer to the reader. Developing empathy for those engaging with the educational materials became a cornerstone of my approach. Working with Francia filled me with delight, satisfaction, and joy, for she had mastered the art of posing straightforward and well-articulated questions pertinent to our students' lives—a quality I have seldom found in other writers.

As we have reflected on our experiences with the SAT and tried to discern its essential components, Gustavo has consistently underscored the pivotal role of visionary individuals who dedicated their lives to advancing projects aimed at enhancing the well-being of others. Earlier, he highlighted some of the contributions of Alberto Alzate, a resolute advocate of the program who spent decades championing the cause of education for rural communities in the department of Risaralda. One can find similar, dedicated individuals in other departments, such as Antioquia and Santander, and we must acknowledge their indispensable role and learn from their examples.

The trajectory of the SAT, with all its intricacies and fluctuations, owes much of its progress to the leadership of these remarkable individuals. When I reflect on their shared characteristics, two fundamental qualities stand out: an unwavering dedication and commitment to the people and places they chose to serve and a profound love that transcended mere rhetoric. This love manifested in their genuine care to look after those who crossed their paths. Their selfless contributions, regarding time and financial resources, played a transformative role in uplifting the rural youth they were devoted to, empowering them to pursue education and serve their communities.

One unforgettable individual in my memory is Álvaro Villa, an extraordinary visionary who navigated the path of pragmatism in his dedication to the farmers of Antioquia, the region in which he resided, aiming to cultivate self-reliance among them. Trained as an engineer, Álvaro demonstrated wisdom in identifying technologies suitable for impoverished farmers and played a pioneering role in appropriate technology—a movement that gained momentum following the publication of E.F. Schumacher's influential work, *"Small is Beautiful"* in 1973.

I first had the privilege of meeting Álvaro in 1984 during my initial visits to various organizations in Colombia and Latin American countries. During this period, we were identifying individuals and organizations engaged in rural education and technology, coinciding with the formation of CELATER, Centro Latinoamericano de Tecnología y Educación Rural—a sister organization led by Farzam and supported by IDRC. I was warmly received in Medellin by María Teresa Restrepo, an exceptional friend associated with Álvaro's recently formed organization, "Comunidad por los Niños." Álvaro and his collaborators were actively establishing and managing demonstration farms in the region, showcasing alternative farming methods and replicable technologies. The main farm was in La Estelaria, land his family had owned for generations.

Álvaro Villa, one of the initiators of SAT in Antioquia

Originating from a relatively well-off family in Antioquia, Álvaro grew up with strong Catholic values and a profound love for humanity. His sensitivity found expression through music, a talent he possessed uniquely. Álvaro radiated a distinctive kind of love, giving selflessly to everyone without expecting anything in return. Despite his simple attire, which he had purposefully adopted, he spoke eloquently, and his home was always open to everyone. Álvaro embodied a renaissance spirit, managing many concepts and practical skills. His true spirituality stemmed from his dedication and love for humanity.

Álvaro saw the potential of the SAT, understanding that his technology and training program could only progress if the population developed the scientific and moral capabilities to actively participate and lead in such work. He became a fervent supporter of the program after Gustavo and I visited Medellin, followed by his visit to Cali, opening doors for collaborations with other organizations in Antioquia.

Regrettably, Álvaro's joyous and fulfilling life met a tragic end in July 1989, deeply intertwined with the reality of the place and the people he devoted his life to. On what seemed like any other day, responding to the needs of those seeking assistance, a dissident guerrilla group lured Álvaro away. Believing they genuinely needed his help, he followed them, and it was the last time his family saw him. The group, thinking Álvaro was wealthy, demanded money that his family did not possess. After a period of ordeal and false hopes, his family received the devastating news that Álvaro had been killed.

But Maria Teresa did not let down the legacy of Álvaro. She gathered a group of extremely dedicated people who were also devoted to education and the environment. She formed an organization, CEIBA, to take forward the work that Comunidad por los Niños had initiated in Antioquia. This organization worked with FUNDAEC for 22 years, formed 70 groups, and trained 120 tutors. The fruits of their work are still present in the remotest areas of Antioquia.

Álvaro Villa (left, in blue shirt); Maria Teresa Restrepo (center, in red jacket), SAT coordinator in Antioquia; Amalia Samper (far right), SAT coordinator in Cundinamarca and Boyacá; with co-workers in Envigado, Antioquia, 1986

A recent conversation with a newfound friend resonates with me as I contemplate the lives of those devoted to the cause of rural education. This individual—who professed her belief that the highest principle in this world was preserving one's own life—posed a question that took me aback. She found it difficult to comprehend the actions of those willing to endure hardships, torture, or even sacrifice their lives for the sake of a cause or principle. According to this person, if presented with the choice to save one's life by renouncing one's beliefs, the most logical course of action would be to do so. Saving oneself, she argued, would allow one to emerge unscathed and continue working towards the betterment of the world. Insisting on maintaining one's principles, in her view, seemed irrational—a choice that would result in one's demise, rendering the deceased body of no utility.

While I acknowledge the merit in her argument, stressing our responsibility for maintaining good health and preserving life, I firmly believe that championing a cause in this world necessitates standing up for one's beliefs and remaining steadfast to one's principles, regardless of the pressures faced. While the term "sacrifice" may not be commonplace in my personal vocabulary, I often contemplate it in the context of individuals capable of forgoing personal comforts for the greater good. I ponder whether we can achieve anything significant in this world without the efforts of those willing to relinquish things dear to them in a given moment for something of greater value, particularly when it has profound implications for the lives of others.

Father Ramón González, a pioneer in the development of SAT in the department of Santander, with two collaborators

Father Jaime Mitchell, long time promoter of SAT, and recognized as the father of rural education in Vélez, Santander

Gathering of 600 SAT students in San Gil, Santander, 1992

A 2024 gathering in Antioquia, from left to right, Nelson Vaca, Haleh Arbab, Gustavo Correa, Father Francisco Ocampo (founder of COREDI), Marta Vergara, Maria Teresa Restrepo (founder of CEIBA), and Ruben Darío Cardona. Nelson, Marta, and Ruben are graduates of FUNDAEC's bachelor's degree program in rural education

Annual gathering of SAT coordinators, Perico Negro, 1990s

Gustavo Correa and Maria Teresa Restrepo together re-visiting the location of the first SAT training in the department of Antioquia many years earlier

Bradley

I can understand how, as you say, Haleh, sacrifice may not enter our personal vocabularies when talking about ourselves. Turning attention to or talking about sacrifices, at a personal level, can look like complaining, dwelling upon problems, or even desiring attention for own efforts. However, when we witness the sacrifices made by others, such as the profound life commitments made by people like Álvaro and many more, we are also moved to use such language to describe them and their actions. People who dedicate themselves to the greater good inspire others to undertake noble acts. Their spirit lives on with us even if the outcome they were striving for, the change they dedicated themselves to, did not materialize in their lifetime. I often think of these special people who dedicate themselves to a goal they know they may never achieve. Through their conduct, such people can inspire others and even entire communities of people to act out of love for what they stood for and sought to accomplish.

Given the depth of the challenges we face in our society today and the centuries it has taken us to get to this point, it is hard to fathom that any of us, any individual in our generation or the next, will see the full fruits of their efforts at social or environmental transformation fully realized. But even if we do not witness the change, it does not mean it will not come or we should not strive. That's why the songs of freedom in the US South, like "We shall overcome… someday," acknowledged the uncertainty of when the change we strive for will arrive and the importance of fortitude in the struggle. When we think of the suffrage movement, the movement for racial healing and justice, or today's efforts to address the climate crisis, the protagonists of movements trying to deliver us to a different future may never see that future realized before they are gone from this earth. What then drives people forward to create the change for the common good they may never see?

I do not believe what drives people like Álvaro or others is merely moral indignation at the ills we face. From personal experience, the people who work selflessly on behalf of others are also some of the most joyful people, and their efforts emanate a love for others. Their purpose is clear, and they derive tremendous happiness from dedication, commitment, and forging ahead to serve future generations. I wonder if that joy comes from feeling truly useful in helping others realize their potential. Sacrifice reminds me of a metaphor that likens someone to a candle whose wax weeps away to keep the flame going.[24] The candle feels it is fulfilling its highest purpose: to keep that flame alive. It gives itself to the flame and transforms itself from solid wax to liquid fuel. In doing so, it slowly disappears, yet the light continues to shine. It is inspiring to see people transform in service as they joyfully dedicate themselves to a cause. It is beautiful and attractive to others, ensuring the flame will remain visible. Seeing their sacrifice emboldens us to find joy in transforming ourselves and keeping the flame going, even if we must give up some comfort. To persevere for generations to come and enjoy the warm vibrancy of a better world is precisely what some of history's most noble, hidden, and under-recognized figures have done for their communities, regions, and humanity.

---

[24] The full quotation, from a talk by 'Abdu'l-Bahá, reads: "Behold a candle, how it gives its light. It weeps its life away drop by drop in order to give forth its flame of light."

A Living Tapestry

FUNDAEC creates conditions for participants to learn and build projects that advance material well-being in their communities and a living tapestry of institutional support as these modest initiatives grow in complexity. FUNDAEC has created a means by which different members of the PSA program in Colombia are united enough to jump at opportunities while maintaining a commitment to action, research, and learning. However, this depends on the shared commitment of individuals and a deep understanding of this distinctive approach.

Bradley Wilson

Opening

As educators, development practitioners, and those engaged in social action are acutely aware: the changes, chances, and crises confronting us in our communities often lead to new challenges, opportunities, or barriers to advancement, which we must overcome. In the context of working in such fields, it is necessary to learn through time that the projects and interventions once envisioned must always evolve to reach a level of sustainability and maintain a meaningful impact on the populations they intend to serve over longer periods. This evolution is never a finished process but the outcome of continual action and reflection. As we've learned through the last few chapters, FUNDAEC's approach to education for development emerged initially out of action research, relationship building, and pedagogical innovation in Norte del Cauca, then grew into a rural educational program, built upon a tutorial learning system (sistema de aprendizaje tutorial, or the SAT) that reached hundreds of communities and tens of thousands of people across Colombia and beyond. New partnerships opened the door to meaningfully expand the scope and reach of FUNDAEC's efforts. The ability to adapt to changing conditions while maintaining a core set of principles and practices was vital to the formation of FUNDAEC and the success and growth of its endeavors.

However, as we see in many contexts around the world, FUNDAEC was not, in these decades of growth, immune to or operating in isolation from challenging social, political, economic, and environmental circumstances. The growth of the SAT occurred amidst a civil conflict in Colombia that created very dangerous circumstances for the communities in which FUNDAEC was working. Political tensions, violent conflict, and the rapid growth of the drug trade are just some of the notable elements of a history within which FUNDAEC was navigating its path of educational innovation. Changes in educational policy; shifting discourses and alliances among higher education institutions, development institutions, and non-profit organizations; resource scarcity; and diverging intellectual and social movements all created an uneven or unstable terrain for the continued growth of the SAT program. We do not dwell here on the details of that history in Colombia except to ground the previous chapters in these pressing realities that touched the lives of many of the collaborators working with FUNDAEC.

In the following conversation, we consider FUNDAEC's focus on capacity building in the late 1990s and 2000s and the effort by FUNDAEC to refine its programming and return to the essence of its approach to education for development: raising a new generation of Promoters of Community Well-being through the development of the Preparation for Social Action program. The development of the PSA program in the 2000s would set FUNDAEC's next steps firmly onto a global path of collaboration.

Bradley

Preparation for Social Action (PSA) is a program now known in many places around the world. What were the circumstances of developing the PSA program?

Gustavo

Before addressing this question of the development of PSA, it is important to go back to the period of greatest growth of the SAT program between 2000 and 2005, as well as the reasons that led us to examine the path taken and its coherence with our vision of the development process and the role of FUNDAEC towards the future. These reflections propelled the creation of the PSA program, Preparation for Social Action, in 2005.

Between 2000 and 2005, the SAT program expanded throughout several departments of Colombia, crossing borders, reaching rural schools supported by the Wong Foundation in Ecuador, the Ngäbe Buglé,

Bri-Bri, and Q'eqchi' indigenous populations of Panama, Costa Rica, and Guatemala, respectively, the Iranduba region in the Brazilian Amazon, and to the rural populations of Honduras and Nicaragua. At one point during this period, there were nearly 50,000 students in the system. In Colombia, in departments such as Antioquia, Tolima, Cundinamarca, Valle del Cauca, Cauca, Santander, and Risaralda, the entire program, with all its components, was legally recognized and became the most promising option to offer a contextualized education, of quality and purpose to rural populations.

The case of the Bayan Association in Honduras and the Padre Fabretto Foundation in Nicaragua in Central America deserves special mention. In Honduras, the Ministry of Education accepted and approved the entire program and made it its national rural education program, fully assuming the payment of tutors and offering lasting support. Currently, it operates with the same vitality and strength as its first years, serving 6,400 active students. In Nicaragua, the process followed the same path as Bayan until, unfortunately, government policies truncated its efforts when, in 2022, about half of the legal status of the country's non-governmental organizations were annulled, among which was the Padre Fabretto Foundation.

FUNDAEC has always admired the dedication and effort of Central American institutions in overcoming obstacles throughout their long journey. Recently, at the SAT meeting in Honduras in May 2024, it was very satisfying to witness the recognition of the protagonists of these stories in Central America and to hear the promises of decisive support from donor institutions. This support ensures that the program—recognized as a vehicle for promoting development in the region—continues to consolidate.

SAT students at Bayan Association, Honduras

SAT students, Wong Foundation, Ecuador

SAT students, Wong Foundation, Ecuador

Visit to Colombia of representatives of the Ministry of Education of Ecuador and Wong Foundation

Visit of Ministry of Education to La Mosquitia, Honduras

SAT students, Padre Fabretto Foundation, Nicaragua

SAT tutors and coordinators, Padre Fabretto Foundation, Nicaragua

SAT students, Talita Kumi Foundation, Guatemala

It should be noted that community support, both in Colombia and elsewhere, was crucial in maintaining the continuity of the program in the face of periodic changes in public officials and their political agendas, which often put financial support at risk. Without the community's determined—and sometimes belligerent—support in defending their children's education, it would have been impossible to guarantee the program's long-term sustainability. Faced with this reality, FUNDAEC had to increase its management capacity to accommodate the growing number of institutions joining the SAT network at both national and international levels. The strategy and challenge were to avoid centralizing growth and instead encourage the expansion of the network.

From the beginning, FUNDAEC recognized that a central element of its development strategy was the creation of management capacity at both individual and institutional levels. Therefore, FUNDAEC had to ensure its growth as an institution remained within reasonable limits while incorporating this aspect into conversations with other institutions. Building the ability within everyone to manage their own affairs and projects is fundamental to a development strategy that seeks to foster autonomy and awaken creativity.

For me, building people's ability to execute is one of the most challenging issues in the field of development. Ideas abound, but execution capacity is scarce and must be developed. We strive to do this by identifying people's potential, accepting them as they are, and being willing to entrust them with responsibilities that may be challenging but are a sure means for their growth. Wisdom has always been crucial in determining the pace and type of support people need at certain times. Often, the results are not seen in the short term, but later, the reward comes with the growth of the individual's and the organization's management capacity.

Among the lessons learned during this period was that emphasizing capacity development made it easier for FUNDAEC and other institutions implementing the SAT in different countries to successfully expand and adapt the program to various contexts.

Much to our regret, the trajectory followed by the SAT program in Colombia was abruptly interrupted. Paradoxically, government laws and regulations in Colombia aimed at facilitating quality education at the national level negatively affected innovative programs aligned with those objectives—as in the case of the SAT. Rules subsequent to the General Education Law 115 of 1994 and Law 715 of 2001 (which determines the modalities of contracting with territorial entities) and other regulatory decrees prevented municipalities and departments from continuing to contract educational services with non-governmental organizations that had not been recognized as formal educational institutions. Private entities that could not join or become formal educational institutions lost their source of financing. They had to abandon, frustrated, the initiatives they had put so much effort into. This was not the only impact the readjustment of laws and regulations regarding rural education had on the program. Unilaterally, without fully understanding the reasons, the SAT was classified as an adult education program—leaving out a large part of the school-age population that the program served.

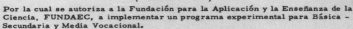

REPUBLICA DE COLOMBIA

MINISTERIO DE EDUCACION NACIONAL

RESOLUCION NUMERÓ 4730 DE 19
(1 8 ABR 1978)

Por la cual se autoriza a la Fundación para la Aplicación y la Enseñanza de la Ciencia, FUNDAEC, a implementar un programa experimental para Básica - Secundaria y Media Vocacional.

EL MINISTRO DE EDUCACION NACIONAL
en ejercicio de sus atribuciones legales, y en especial
de las que le concede el Decreto 088 de 1976, y

CONSIDERANDO:

Que el Ministerio de Educación Nacional está interesado en el desarrollo y experimentación de Programas educativos que se identifiquen con las necesidades de la población rural del país,

Que dichos programas deben estar encaminados hacia la elaboración de un curriculum que prepare personas capaces de integrar los conocimientos y destrezas de varias disciplinas para dar soluciones a las necesidades básicas del campesino,

Que la Fundación para la Aplicación y la Enseñanza de la Ciencia, FUNDAEC, es una institución de enseñanza e investigación en educación rural cuyos programas integran disciplinas en función de las necesidades de las zonas rurales,

Que esta Institución cuenta en este momento con instalaciones propias en la vereda de La Arrobleda, Municipio de Santander de Quilichao, Departamento del Cauca, donde está educando un grupo de jóvenes provenientes de las áreas rurales vecinas y de diferente escolaridad, algunos de los cuales están ya tomando cursos universitarios,

Que las experiencias de FUNDAEC son de mucho interés para el diseño de los nuevos programas curriculares que adelanta la Dirección de Diseño y Programación Curricular de Educación Formal,

RESUELVE:

ARTICULO 1o. - Autorízase a la Fundación para la Aplicación y la Enseñanza de la Ciencia, FUNDAEC, para llevar a cabo un programa experimental para áreas rurales a nivel de educación media, con el objeto de preparar agentes de bienestar rural capaces de dar soluciones integradas apropiadas para las necesidades del pequeño agricultor.

ARTICULO 2o. - La primera etapa del programa experimental que adelantará la Fundación para la Aplicación y la Enseñanza de - la Ciencia, FUNDAEC, tendrá una duración de tres años, al cabo de los cua

Dupls. Minaduoación.

Resolution 4730 from the Colombian Ministry of Education recognizing SAT as an educational innovation, April 1978

FUNDAEC immensely valued the contributions of all these organizations, which, despite having to limit their actions, played a crucial role in improving rural education in Colombia. FUNDAEC takes pride in having contributed to the education of thousands of young people in Colombia and in having influenced policies concerning rural education. It is also satisfying to observe that, in the regions where the SAT operated, there remains a critical mass of educated individuals who, wherever they may be, continue to defend the ideals of rural education for development. Despite these circumstances, demand for the program persisted, and in other countries, such as Honduras, the SAT prospered.

Haleh

At that time, there was a significant demand for the SAT program, not only within Colombia or Latin America but also in other parts of the world. Consequently, we found ourselves reflecting on the core principles of the program, its accomplishments, and its replicable aspects. It was evident to everyone that this program was fundamentally oriented towards development, firmly situated within the domain of what is commonly known as education for development. The SAT program had successfully secured accreditation from governments, a noteworthy achievement that greatly benefited many students and tutors. However, this accreditation was considered a secondary focus compared to the program's main objectives.

While accreditation brought numerous advantages, it also brought a set of disadvantages. In regions where the program received governmental financial and moral support, it provided stability, particularly in ensuring tutors' remuneration. However, this support came with constraints, subjecting the program to the political will of regional and national governments. Moreover, complying with the demands of ministries—who often failed to grasp the essence of the content: FUNDAEC's concept of curricular integration, and the program's purpose—forced organizations to incorporate courses that did not align with the original conception and pedagogy. This process consumed considerable time and energy, with the added challenge that these additions were sometimes counterproductive.

During our comprehensive evaluation of the program's achievements, we deliberated on the significance of downplaying its academic degree aspect. Would participants still be motivated to engage? Would the program maintain its success and positive effects if it placed less emphasis on formal credentials? These were crucial questions guiding our discussions.

To address the question of motivation, we revisited our fundamental assumptions about human nature, and the driving forces behind individuals' pursuit of learning and the efforts they exert to build a better world. FUNDAEC has consistently recognized two motivating forces that propel individuals to acquire knowledge and contribute to enhancing society: a thirst for knowledge and an attraction to beauty. The content of our program has always aimed to resonate with these innate aspects of human nature, seeking to evoke and enhance the attraction to beauty and to intensify the thirst for knowledge.

PSA students in Córdoba and Bolívar, Colombia

Our observations reminded us that students were most motivated when they perceived their learning as a means to enhance their understanding of the world, providing practical benefits for their lives, families, and communities. With these insights and drawing upon our long-standing convictions, we took the bold step of freeing ourselves, to a certain extent, from the demands of offering a program focused on attaining an academic degree. We realized that by doing so, everything else would remain unchanged—the curriculum, the tutor, the group dynamics, the coordination structure, the relationship with the community, and the implementing organization.

Gustavo

Haleh mentioned the fundamental reasons why what we called the SAT program was transformed into the PSA program (Preparation for Social Action), which was the question Bradley posed at the beginning. Freed from the straitjacket of meeting the requirements of Colombia's Ministry of Education and the perception of the SAT program as equivalent to secondary education, we were able to return to the essence of the program, which was to create capacity in a population to be the main protagonist of its development. This process began with thinking about training individuals who could become 'community development catalysts'; rather than educating people in a certain profession, the idea was to educate and train them to become increasingly capable of acting effectively within their social environment. The program then began to be called Preparation for Social Action, preserving the main elements— the texts, the group, and the concept of a tutor—and returned to its original purpose.

Supported by the Hewlett Foundation, through a project aimed at scaling up successful educational experiences, FUNDAEC helped gradually establish the PSA program in Africa and the Pacific. It centered on individuals committed to social action, including Selam Ahderom and Debbie Singh in Uganda, Garth and Karen Pollock in Zambia, Tiati a Zock and Gideon Tem in Cameroon, and Jalal Mills and Alphy Gononua in Papua New Guinea. Organizations like Rays of Light in Vanuatu soon began adopting the PSA, signifying its growing influence. Building a network of relationships with continuous guidance and support from FUNDAEC, as had been successfully demonstrated in Colombia, became vital for nurturing institutional capacity and the exchange of learning. Annual meetings were instrumental in clarifying concepts and coordinating efforts to tailor the experience to these new settings. At the same time, regular visits from FUNDAEC staff significantly enhanced the training of local staff, field coordinators, and tutors.

Training of PSA tutors, Papua New Guinea

Training of PSA tutors, Uganda

Training of PSA tutors, Zambia

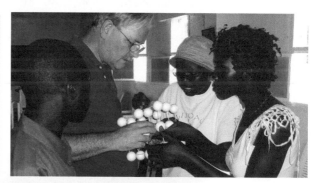

PSA training in Colombia with participants from different countries

Promoting autonomy in each institution addressed the challenges inherent in geographical distance and costs. As expected, when a program is transferred prematurely, new situations arise that we must address to remain faithful to the principles under which the program was conceived.

Preserving the integrity of an experience initially conceived within conditions that are difficult to replicate is a considerable challenge. Attempting to replicate the experience across various environments and for different audiences heightened this difficulty. Understanding and implementing the operational structure, such as having a central team essential for learning, is relatively straightforward. However, selecting the appropriate individuals to lead this effort remains a complicated task, regardless of the nature of the program. It is often necessary to modify the original experience to enable its transfer while maintaining the program's fundamental principles. Yet, these changes come with the risk that the experience may alter to the point where it no longer reflects its initial intent.

Nonetheless, apprehension about deviating from the original concept should not prevent us from investigating new applications for an educational experience. Often, openness to different approaches can reveal opportunities previously unconsidered. For instance, aspects of a program designed for a particular group may benefit another. An excellent example of successful application and transformation is Kimanya-Ngeyo, an organization that has been implementing the Preparation for Social Action (PSA) program in Uganda since 2007. Recognizing the teachers' critical role in developing the intellectual and moral capacities of the young and enabling them to contribute to society's improvement, Kimanya began a year-long training program in 2015. Guided by Joey Lample, who brought his deep understanding of the SAT program in Honduras from his doctoral work, the program started with primary teachers. It later included secondary school teachers in Jinja and

Teacher training, Kimanya-Ngeyo Foundation, Uganda

Buikwe districts. The training utilized selected texts from the PSA program and supplementary materials addressing pedagogical issues.

A randomized evaluation of this professional development program suggested that the teachers' engagement with these texts significantly affected their pedagogical methods, which, in turn, dramatically improved student learning.[25] Students of these teachers performed better than their peers in official examinations. These findings reaffirmed the value of our work over the years, particularly the systematic approach to learning contained within these texts, which holds promise for future educational initiatives.

Bradley

When I listen to the arc of the story of the educational work of FUNDAEC, I hear a multi-step process that first moves from Norte del Cauca to regions throughout Colombia, and then another, moving from Colombia to other areas of Latin America, and later on, to other parts of the world. This growth process demonstrates how you encountered challenges and the interweaving of new networks and relationships. One of the things I have learned through years of development work is that establishing new relationships impresses upon us the need to communicate and come to an agreement on the intentions of any endeavor. In the steps taken at this time in the reach of the SAT and later the PSA programs, there was an opportunity to do that with people concerned about the development of the regions where they lived and worked. Certainly, these contexts were similar to Colombia from the standpoint of the desire for effective rural educational programming. Yet, of course, the context differed from place to place.

From a more conceptual standpoint, this discussion about scaling up and adapting these educational programs had me thinking about how FUNDAEC has navigated the relationship between the abstract and concrete elements of its approach, the rigid and flexible aspects of the curriculum, and the universal and particular principles that shaped its educational programs. This tension seemed to be ever-present in the thinking of FUNDAEC. It is also a central tension in the field of development and education itself. In the development field, there is this persistent critique of the universal application of certain ideas, techniques, and approaches across the globe and their imposition through particular institutions, packages, and programs. Likewise, there is concern about relativism and particularisms that essentialize certain groups' ideas, techniques, or approaches but reach certain limits in fostering wider unities across differences. A similar tension exists in

---

[25] Ashraf, N., Banerjee, A. and Nourani, V. (2023) *Learning to teach by learning to learn.* [Unpublished working paper]. University of Chicago and Makerere University.

educational efforts where standards of learning and achievement seek to be universal. At the same time, both teachers and students live within the particularity of their own experiences, unique needs, and potentialities.

Nevertheless, not all people see these tensions similarly. Some may see the SAT or the PSA as just another educational program or development intervention to fit into an established model or replace an existing initiative. Sometimes, it gets a little messy in people's minds because our social realities are so challenging, and we seek a response or resolution to our needs, and a program like the SAT or PSA might appear to resolve those needs. For instance, in response to the need to provide rural education, promote material in a community, or confront the disintegrative forces in society, many folks who desire to make a difference are looking around and trying to find a simple solution or an answer to the question: "what do we do?" They are searching for a program or package—an understandable point of view given how education and development fields have operated conventionally. I just mean to note that by holding this productive tension in mind and understanding the creative synthesis presented by the sistema de aprendizaje tutorial and its operation in a given place, it enables us to see the SAT and PSA as a means—not an end—to fostering participation in the development process of a region. It is a means to certain ends, not an end to apply as a programmatic solution.

What I hear from you describing the history of the SAT and the PSA is that FUNDAEC is still acting and reflecting on its experience, even 50 years down this path. It is still working from this approach. In the mid-2000s—given both the newfound network of institutions collaborating in different regions and the barriers to its continued expansion in its current form in Colombia—how was FUNDAEC ensuring its new partners understood the prerequisite principles and practices? How, for instance, did the concept of a pyramid of community workers and the central protagonist in the program—the promoter of community well-being— evolve or become clearer in the minds of FUNDAEC at this time?

Haleh

When navigating scenarios aligning with what individuals in the development or education field might classify as scaling up, transference, or replication of an experience, program, or technology, FUNDAEC recognized the inherent challenges posed by cultural, infrastructural, and socioeconomic differences between contexts. Understanding the necessity of adapting the program to suit specific needs and conditions in new environments, FUNDAEC acknowledged the importance of flexibility. This flexibility extended to modifying teaching methods and strategies, or introducing additional materials when necessary—all without compromising the program's integrity. Consequently, FUNDAEC consistently integrated action, research, and learning elements into its work. Throughout these endeavors, persistent questions surfaced: What accomplishments can we attribute to this experience? What are the critical success factors? Which components or principles of the program are non-negotiable—essential elements that significantly contribute to success and should be retained even in scaled-up or transferred versions?

One aspect that has consistently set FUNDAEC apart is its distinctive approach to releasing human potentialities—a concept we've referenced multiple times in our discussions—that includes action, research, and learning. This approach has been integral to FUNDAEC's work since its inception. When delving into topics like the SAT or the PSA, it is essential to incorporate this aspect of our work into the conversation. Unlike merely composing a series of books based on perceived needs, FUNDAEC's approach encompasses continuous endeavors to improve specific aspects of local life, addressing the capabilities individuals need to develop to reinforce change effectively. The texts and the program stem from these efforts, incorporating lessons learned from actions taken into the educational materials, program design, and structure. This approach also influences the content and format of the training provided for those tasked with implementing the program.

Capacity building is a critical concept essential for program sustainability and successful replication. It necessitates investing in the training of individuals to implement the program in new settings, as well as of local staff or stakeholders to ensure a solid grasp of its principles and methodologies. FUNDAEC has consistently prioritized capacity building, evident in its training initiatives associated with implementing the SAT and the PSA and through the university program in rural education.

Speaking of capacity building, I'd like to share a case related to the University Center and its administration. It illustrates the complexity of finding prepared individuals and the necessity of cultivating talent within FUNDAEC. During the establishment of the University, as we worked on organizing structures and administration, we sought to hire someone with training in administration. We were fortunate to find a young man who had completed his master's at a prestigious university in Cali. Though initially reluctant about traveling to the rural area outside Cali, where the University Center was, he accepted the position. Collaboratively, we endeavored to set up the system.

However, after two weeks, he approached me one morning expressing regret, stating, "I am truly sorry, but I can't continue with this. I have been offered another position. What you're doing is noble, but it's not for me, and I don't believe it will be easy to persuade others like me to take on such a role. It demands too much commitment. I think the only way forward is to train people within FUNDAEC. Take a few students in your program and set up the system to suit your needs." His advice was thoughtful, and we parted on amicable terms. Following his suggestion, I trained a select group of our students, and these individuals, among others, are the ones who continue to uphold and drive FUNDAEC forward today.

20th Anniversary Celebration of Centro Universitario de Bienestar Rural, Perico Negro, 2009

Bradley

Working with FUNDAEC, I have seen this talent and the capacities you referred to among the individuals within the organization. One reflection that I can offer from my experience with the PSA program is the capacity I have witnessed among tutors, coordinators, and others within FUNDAEC's team that enables it to grow in its impact over time, but also to grow rapidly as more and more people at the grassroots express a desire to participate. This capacity reflects the deep understanding of the program's purpose, practical factors, and the system's essential elements—tutor, group, and texts—that emerged over the past decades. As you described, Haleh, since FUNDAEC had raised the internal group together to guide the work, the team has been able to adapt responsively to and build upon what is being learned in the field of action as the program advances at the community level. All participants are engaged in the enterprise of learning how to serve their communities in meaningful, purposeful, and effective ways.

One of the elements I find so inspiring about FUNDAEC is its capacity to continuously grow the PSA program in Colombia. From my observation, this is enabled by the formation of capacity at the local scale and a level of commitment to support that local development, which is quite unparalleled, in my estimation. Working with FUNDAEC, I have been impressed by its administrative capacity, which facilitates the flow of observations, knowledge, analysis, consultation, and recommendations to move freely and nimbly across regions to support the advancement and evolution of the PSA program.

Gathering of PSA coordinators from Colombia, Perico Negro, 2016

This institutional capacity is a hallmark of FUNDAEC's vision for developing individual and communal capacity. FUNDAEC creates conditions for participants to learn and build projects that advance material well-being in their communities and a living tapestry of institutional support as these modest initiatives grow in complexity. FUNDAEC has created a means by which different members of the PSA program in Colombia are united enough to jump at opportunities while maintaining a commitment to action, research, and learning. However, this depends on the shared commitment of individuals and a deep understanding of this distinctive approach.

Releasing Human Potentialities

*The enterprise that came to be identified as La Fundación
para la Aplicación y Enseñanza de la Ciencia (FUNDAEC)
aimed to pave the way for individuals to cultivate their abilities
and realize the collective aspiration of a dignified future...
Spanning half a century, this mission and the practical steps we
have taken to realize it have become a testament to the enduring
hope that FUNDAEC will perpetually evolve and its champions
will rise to meet this fundamental need.*

Haleh Arbab

Opening

One important theme threading its way through our conversations about FUNDAEC is its distinctive approach to education and development, which has propelled and guided its work. Our concern with elaborating on this approach stems from the challenge of presenting FUNDAEC's work in the context of a world with continuous fragmentation of spheres of intellectual activity, specialization of educational training, segmentation of development practice, and disintegration of social life. Everything, it seems, is fragmented in our minds. For instance, in different quarters, FUNDAEC might be merely represented as an educational institution, a research center, a development organization, or even a project manager, depending on the orientation of the assessment. This fragmentation and the desire to maintain boundaries between these different spheres of activity hinder a deeper understanding of FUNDAEC's approach to releasing human potentialities. In this chapter, we navigate this fragmentation and attempt to weave together the philosophical, methodological, pedagogical, and practical elements of FUNDAEC's approach into a coherent whole.

One of the challenges with describing any given approach in a book or text—rather than witnessing or embodying it firsthand as it unfolds over time—is the challenge of reductionism or oversimplification and the assumption that reading alone offers a sufficient glimpse into its inner workings. However, we hope that, given the histories shared in the conversation thus far and the 50-year arc of FUNDAEC's work, the challenge of reductionism presents less of a concern. If the reader has made it this far, they will have recognized that this is no mere intellectual project. Throughout this book, we have attempted to foreground FUNDAEC's approach in a greater context for the reader's benefit.

Reviewing the Threadwork

Let's return to the thread work we have done thus far. We began our conversation by telling stories of our unique backgrounds that led us to work in development. The people who collaborate with FUNDAEC have a strong sense of commitment to place and to one another that exceeds what may be found in many intellectual projects. Gustavo began with a passion for mathematics but shifted towards development work after being introduced to multidisciplinary discussions on rural development and building relationships with the people of Norte del Cauca. Haleh's commitment to Colombia stemmed from childhood dreams, eventually leading her to forge deep connections with the land and its people. Bradley's interest in development sparked as a teenager in Central America, and he later dedicated himself to studying and working in Nicaragua and West Virginia. Despite our diverse paths, we share a commitment to understanding and serving the communities and regions we call home. Our own stories emphasize a characteristic of FUNDAEC's collaborators: the importance of long-term engagement in development efforts rooted in mutual aid and building solidarities with people who live in those places.

Throughout the conversation, we have also noted that FUNDAEC stresses the importance of combating any sense of superiority and appreciating the diversity of knowledges within rural communities. FUNDAEC's champions acknowledge the limitations of their understanding and expertise, advocating for a humble posture and a deeper immersion in community life. This approach contrasts with conventional development methodologies, which often presume to diagnose problems and provide solutions without fully understanding the local context or involving community members in decision-making. As Gustavo said in our earlier conversations, "At the heart of our approach...the cornerstone was a constant dialogue of knowledges, an essential element for bridging differences and jointly constructing something of great significance." He then explained that "our approach recognized that all could contribute to knowledge in their way based on their language, background, and experience" and that "we sought to create an approach founded on the principles of embracing and valuing diversity while upholding the knowledge and experiences of each participant."

The cornerstone of a dialogue of knowledges shaped the development of FUNDAEC's focus on learning processes and education. The development of its educational content and pedagogy sought to elevate the dignity of its participants and instill a sense of service and commitment among young people, empowering them with research skills and the ability to design collective initiatives to enhance the well-being of their communities. FUNDAEC emphasized the importance of integrating education with development initiatives and promoting skills beyond specific areas of expertise. Yet, rather than just focusing on developing and delivering curricular materials, it saw the need to establish new institutions and centers of learning in the region. The concept of a sistema de aprendizaje tutorial formed the basis for a scalable educational model adaptable to diverse rural conditions. The success of the SAT (the sistema de aprendizaje tutorial) demonstrated the potential for organic growth and sustainable expansion. Through the SAT, FUNDAEC introduced a novel approach to rural education, elevating the quality of education in rural areas previously considered too costly, difficult, and improbable to achieve.

Yet FUNDAEC's work did not end there. We also highlighted FUNDAEC's concerns with balancing a principled focus on its core mission while maintaining a pace of organic growth as it scaled up its programs. As the sistema de aprendizaje tutorial spread across Colombia and then to other countries in Latin America, FUNDAEC faced the challenge of ensuring that the essential principles and practices were understood and upheld by new partners while allowing for necessary adaptations to fit local needs and conditions. As we discussed, the tension between the abstract and the concrete, the universal and the particular, had been a central consideration for FUNDAEC. This tension is inherent in development and education, where there is often a push for universal approaches alongside the recognition of local context and diversity. FUNDAEC navigated this tension by emphasizing flexibility in its programs, allowing for adaptations while safeguarding core principles. The sistema de aprendizaje tutorial—the tutor, texts, and group—embodied in the SAT and later the PSA served as a flexible framework that could be tailored to diverse contexts while maintaining essential elements.

Capacity building emerged as a critical aspect of FUNDAEC's approach, not only among the participants at the grassroots level but also in ensuring program sustainability and successful replication through tutor training and coordination. FUNDAEC invested in training individuals to implement the programs in new settings, ensuring a solid understanding of the underlying principles and methodologies. This investment in capacity building across a pyramid of Promoters of Community Well-being enabled FUNDAEC to cultivate its talent pool from the ground up and build a network of skilled individuals committed to the organization's vision. By investing in its students and providing them with opportunities to lead and innovate, FUNDAEC ensured the sustainability of its programs.

In what follows, we have asked Haleh to elaborate on FUNDAEC's approach to development, education, and research. One might say an approach is more than a mere method. An approach includes moral intentions, philosophical assumptions, methodological considerations, and experiential qualities that guide a process of inquiry and action. FUNDAEC uses the term distinctive approach, rather than methodology, to signal a wider and more encompassing array of intellectual and social practices related to the generation and application of knowledge. To say that FUNDAEC—or any development institution—has a distinctive approach, in other words, is not a simple matter. Efforts to promote development around the world are shaped by certain intellectual tendencies, habits of mind, ways of being and knowing, and methodologies that guide the behavior of individuals and institutions. Moreover, an approach, when considered as a manifold of interrelated intellectual and social practices, can have a significant bearing on what one does: one's sense of purpose, the conceptualization of development itself, the adoption or deployment of particular scientific methodologies, the design of educational processes, the formulation of particular questions, ideas, and plans, and of course the results or outcomes of that action.

The ways that FUNDAEC's protagonists think about this question of approach emerged in the context of significant intellectual debates about the participation of people in development, the nature and role of science in society, the purpose of education and research, and the relationship between individuals, institutions, and communities as they pursue higher levels of spiritual and material wellbeing. After this philosophical, methodological, and pedagogical introduction to the core themes, we return together to synthesize these ideas into the framework through which FUNDAEC operates: the formation of groups and the establishment of cycles of action-reflection, study, and consultation. This intellectual and practical approach to development is an enduring feature of FUNDAEC's weaving work.

Haleh Arbab

I have long held that one characteristic that sets FUNDAEC apart from other organizations is its distinctive approach to development. I acknowledge the challenge of encapsulating this approach in writing—an arduous and almost insurmountable task. I am nonetheless inspired by the hope of conveying some semblance of this vital yet subtle aspect of this work to the reader in this chapter.

The distinctive approach described below, I believe, has been the undercurrent of FUNDAEC's philosophy and the values its champions hold dear. Often implicit, it has continually shaped its decisions and behaviors, influencing intangible features such as attitudes, motivations, and organizational cultural norms. Though not overtly expressed, these qualities govern its perception and prioritization of problems, as well as its method selection. The approach has provided a backdrop for adaptable yet ethically grounded action. It has subtly directed both interpersonal dynamics and the long-term trajectory of its projects. While the methods and strategies have provided a visible structure for action, the approach has been a less noticeable layer; it has driven innovation and ensured that every facet of its work is in harmony with a deeper vision and purpose, thus serving as a foundation for day-to-day practices and overarching objectives.

Those of us who have worked closely with FUNDAEC have been firmly convinced throughout these years that our approach and methodology must align with the institution's fundamental purpose, which is to contribute to the betterment of the communities it serves. This conviction compels us to continually recall that our primary aim is not to engage in scientific research or to seek academic recognition in the sciences. Similarly, we are not driven by corporate objectives of product and service enhancement. Although these pursuits are legitimate and pertinent under different circumstances, our commitment lies in a complex set of activities designed to enable change in the lives of the populations with whom we work.

To better understand FUNDAEC's approach, it is important to consider some characteristics that ensure alignment with and support its overarching aim. I am not referring to the specific methods or techniques for individual project tasks. Although these methods stem from an overall approach and must resonate with it, they are adaptable and tailored to meet the unique demands of each initiative engaged in. I intend to outline the essential attributes of the broad strategy, which serves as the context for these methods. A key attribute is that all these endeavors should encourage a continual learning process.

Learning, a term closely associated with acquiring knowledge, holds significant value in contemporary discourse. Yet, the pressing question remains: who are the learners, what are they learning, and for what purpose? This query is not superficial; it demands thorough analysis. In FUNDAEC, we have consistently maintained that the people themselves are not just the primary agents of change but also the principal learners. The knowledge created ought to be pertinent to their needs and applicable to enhancing their lives and those of the people in their region. And yet, FUNDAEC has always eschewed simplistic binaries that categorize the world into oppressors and oppressed, rich and poor, redeemed and condemned, modern and backward, the industrious and the idle. Such reductive dichotomies find no place in the fabric of our work. The concept of the oneness of humankind underscores the vision of the world we strive to create. Thus, when we engage in development projects, we recognize ourselves as part of the collective—a group, community, or population directly impacted by these initiatives. Our participation is characterized more by emotional connection, shared attitudes, and dedication than mere physical presence.

Repeatedly, in FUNDAEC's texts, we have challenged the view of development as a transactional exchange from the 'developed' to the 'underdeveloped' or as simple acts of charity and service provision. We advocate for a perspective of development as a collective effort that sparks structural change across society's mental, institutional, social, and cultural dimensions. In this vein of development, agents of change embark on an educational expedition, uncovering the myriad of nuanced, interconnected dynamics that orchestrate comprehensive societal change and mastering the strategies necessary to facilitate these changes.

However, this raises a further question: How does this concept offer fresh perspectives that set it apart from established development paradigms, and what distinctive contributions might it offer to enrich the broader discourse and practices in the development field? One way to address this question is by examining the concept of participation, which has been central to development discourse. Without delving into a detailed analysis of the various dimensions of this concept, I will highlight a few perspectives on participation as approached by different thinkers and practitioners in the field.

At its most basic level, participation can be seen as mobilization. Clearly, any effort to improve individual and social well-being necessitates mobilizing people to actively engage in initiatives aimed at these goals. For example, mobilization is important in campaigns focused on improving the health of a population, as is evident in vaccination efforts. However, since the days that FUNDAEC came into existence, people have recognized that participation in development involves more than just mobilizing individuals for projects.

A second concern of participation is related to a sense of ownership. Development organizations have always sought to foster participation that enhances the local population's sense of project ownership. It is widely accepted that ownership is bolstered when people contribute their time, materials, and labor. This was especially clear in past projects that introduced specific technologies to communities.

During my master's thesis research in various rural communities in Guatemala, I focused on local participation in projects advocating for Lorena stoves. These stoves aim to eliminate harmful kitchen smoke and reduce wood consumption. It was observed that community members who were involved in building the stoves tended to maintain them better. Yet, this involvement did not always result in the stoves being appropriately used, with many well-constructed stoves left unused as people reverted to traditional cooking methods. The literature of that era documented many instances where active community participation in constructing schools, wells, or healthcare centers did not necessarily engender a sense of ownership.

I recall a story that Father Jaime Mitchell—known as the father of rural education in Velez, Santander, and a staunch promoter of the SAT—shared with me. He realized the true meaning of participation when, one stormy night, a group of parents knocked on his door. They came to tell him that the roof of 'his' school, which they felt they had only helped build, had collapsed. These stories and similar observations emphasized that simple participation, through mobilization or contribution in labor and kind, was insufficient for sustainable development. While mobilization around specific issues was important, genuine sustainability demanded that a sense of ownership be established within the community. The secret to fostering this ownership was to make projects community-driven, involving community members at every stage—from identifying needs and implementing projects, to evaluating their outcomes.

The third concern of participation, therefore, was to consider ways of developing techniques for assessing community needs. This was a concern of many in the development field in the 1980s and continues today. When community needs were pinpointed, community members were urged to collaboratively determine how to address them. Stories emerged, for example, of communities prioritizing a soccer field over educational, agricultural, or health projects. The underlying lesson was that supporting communities in meeting their perceived needs was an essential first step, setting the stage for broader, more impactful projects to improve their social and economic conditions. By embracing a community-driven approach, community members were not only mobilized and given ownership of the development process but also recognized as vital contributors. This approach ensured that their preferences and priorities were taken seriously, transforming them into active agents in the quest for social and economic advancement.

These three insights about participation from development practice were significant, reflecting a rich tapestry of experiences. The conclusions reached through the efforts of practitioners working in communities were cogent and resonant with extensive practical knowledge. Yet, from the standpoint of FUNDAEC, the concept of participation was more profound. We came to see it as intimately linked to education. We learned that genuine participation—integral to a community's development—required an educational process seamlessly integrating traditional and contemporary knowledge. Other chapters of this book address this subject, so I will not reiterate it here. Suffice it to say that FUNDAEC understood participation as a dynamic process in which individuals actively create and apply knowledge. Fostering the participation of groups and communities in their paths of development—in ways that do not constantly depend upon charismatic leaders, professional researchers, or development experts—calls for an adequate educational foundation that releases their limitless potential.

To direct attention to this question of releasing the potential of individuals and communities, FUNDAEC concluded that we also needed to consider the quality of participation. What I call participation quality—a notion not easily quantified—relates to the essence or intrinsic attributes of things, distinct from mere frequency of occurrence. In FUNDAEC's work with communities, the 'quality of participation' carries a nuanced and profound meaning. Distinguishing this quality from more superficial forms of engagement requires reflection. It is not a concept that lends itself to easy description or simple metrics.

As I see it, the quality of participation is deeply entwined with the attributes of those involved—representatives of FUNDAEC and community members. It's about more than just showing up; it's about fostering a symbiotic relationship where understanding and an unwritten accord exist to honor values like integrity, respect, and a shared commitment to collective growth. Such high-quality participation moves beyond individualistic aims or seeking accolades. It involves recognizing and valuing each person's contributions within a framework of common goals. It is about nurturing a culture where engagement is driven not by self-interest but by an authentic will to contribute to the common good, to learn from each other, and to work collaboratively towards shared aspirations.

In this light, a unified dedication to these ideals and a concerted endeavor to live by these principles—which cultivate a milieu that harmonizes communal welfare and individual progress—characterizes the essence of participation within FUNDAEC's community interactions. This shared dedication ensures that participation is not just about involvement but about meaningful engagement that enriches both the individual and the collective. FUNDAEC's philosophy addresses a pervasive contradiction in societal attitudes: both expecting populations to be catalysts for change and to take the lead in societal transformation and, at the same time, the detrimental tendency to limit them to simplistic notions and information, reserving more complex material for a select intellectual few. This dichotomy often leads to the dissemination of oversimplified and biased information, reducing it to propaganda.

FUNDAEC distinguishes itself by its faith in the broader population's ability to grasp and engage with complex concepts and reasoning. Nonetheless, this view does not romanticize the masses but emphasizes why education is central to FUNDAEC's mission. If, as Gustavo noted earlier, the dialogue of knowledges forms the cornerstone of FUNDAEC's approach, then its educational processes must elevate such a dialogue. If fostering the participation of more and more people in the generation, application, and diffusion of knowledge is necessary for meaningful societal progress, then—according to FUNDAEC—an appropriate education system would need to be created. However, achieving such a goal is no simple matter. There are many potential pitfalls and cul-de-sacs. FUNDAEC also needed to consider how to maintain a commitment to seeing the great potentialities of people and to sustain hope in accompanying them as they reach for greater spiritual and material wellbeing, creating an educational process that could carry the responsibility of such an ambitious goal as well as considering other conceptual elements.

I wish to revisit a core principle that shapes FUNDAEC's understanding of the social and material world: the notion of reality's inherent unity. To honor a commitment to wholeness, we have diligently examined the concepts and narratives we use to interpret and describe the world. In other words, our commitment to wholeness has many implications for everything we do. Our perception of the world, assumptions about what is knowable and achievable, and the mental categories we employ when encountering phenomena greatly shape how we comprehend and articulate our social reality. In this context, our theoretical insights stand as the primary framework guiding the organization of our empirical knowledge.

As Bradley introduces in the preface to the book, describing the great divides that characterize our present conditions in the world—between generations, the breach in rural and urban life, the gap between rich and poor, and our separation from nature through industrial change—the threat of fragmentation, divisiveness, and compartmentalization in all facets of life is both real and palpable. In many ways, one can fall victim to believing this fragmentation is a fundamental, inescapable, and predestined reality chaining humanity.

At FUNDAEC, we believe in and are committed to an integrated reality. The world is not essentially fragmented. We understand reality as a unified entity, a totality. This belief, rooted in the teachings of Bahá'u'lláh (the founder of the Bahá'í Faith), has found further resonance in the insights provided by David Bohm, a brilliant physicist, and philosopher whose ideas have significantly influenced FUNDAEC's approach to knowledge generation.

Bohm,[26] a proponent of the wholeness of reality, explored the relationship between thoughts about reality and reality itself. He uncovered a profound connection between the fragmentation of the human mind and the societal fragmentation prevalent today. A fragmented mind formulates fragmented questions about reality, resulting in fragmented answers and contributing to the construction of a human society fragmented not only in individual and collective thought but also in the organization of human affairs. According to Bohm, this fragmentation "[leads] to a kind of general confusion of the mind, which creates an endless series of problems and interferes with our clarity of perception so seriously as to prevent us from being able to solve most of them."

Yet, it is also crucial to note that Bohm recognizes the practicality of dealing with specific aspects of reality separately. The human mind naturally divides and separates to manage problems effectively, a practice rooted in humanity's earliest history and the realization that humans are not identical to nature. This realization allowed for autonomy in human thinking, surpassing some of the limits imposed by nature. However, taking this necessary process of separation and division to extremes is one of the problems of the workings of the fragmented mind. Another problem is what Bohm called an almost universal habit of taking the content of our thoughts for a description of the world as it is—the tendency to read thought as directly corresponding to objective reality. This habit leads us to look at our arbitrary divisions as real, and the world is therefore seen and experienced as broken up into fragments.

Our acknowledgment of the world's inherent wholeness and an awareness that our descriptions may not fully capture the reality we aim to represent has been crucial in avoiding the pitfalls associated with a fragmented mindset. In the development field, this type of thinking is prone to creating divisions and distinctions, offering solutions for isolated issues, and mistaking constructed categories for the ultimate truth. We have consciously pursued a holistic perspective, accepting that

---

[26] Bohm, D. (1980/2003) *Wholeness and the implicate order.* New York: Routledge.

while division may occasionally arise, it is only temporary. The next step involves placing these fragments within the larger context of reality. This approach allows us to discover new unities and forge connections between seemingly disparate elements.

It is important to realize that we can only maintain the wholeness of our approach if we eliminate the pervasive dichotomy between theory and practice that spans multiple disciplines and creates a chasm that can hinder both progress and the application of knowledge. In education, many pedagogical theories fail to translate into classroom strategies, leaving educators struggling to apply abstract concepts to their students' diverse and immediate needs. In the medical field, a significant disconnect exists between clinical research and the populations it aims to benefit. A one-way flow of information, where insights and findings from research fail to consider the practical realities faced by patients and healthcare providers, exacerbates this divide. Similarly, in environmental policy, the complex models and predictions offered by science often encounter roadblocks when it comes to practical implementation, as political, economic, and social factors complicate their translation into actionable policies. This theory-practice gap underscores the necessity for a more integrated approach that bridges these divides with effective communication, interdisciplinary collaboration, and a commitment to ongoing learning and adaptation in the face of real-world challenges.

Robert Chambers described the gap between theory and practice in rural development many years ago as a division between those who analyze and those who act, between those he calls "academics" and "practitioners." At one pole, we have academic, social scientists preoccupied with the 'what?' and 'why?' of development and underdevelopment and with political economy—who gets what, why and how, and the processes which determine their answers; and at the other pole, we have practical administrators and technical scientists who concern themselves with the 'how?' of development, with trying to change things, and with trying to get things done. According to Chambers, the physical, linguistic, and experiential distance between these two groups is wide, and they often have little sympathy or communication. To hear a seminar at a university about modes of production in the morning and then attend a meeting in a government office about agricultural extension in the afternoon leaves a schizoid feeling; one might not know that both refer to the same small farmers and might doubt whether either discussion had anything to contribute to the other.[27]

In FUNDAEC, we have tried throughout the years to contribute to closing this gap. Our invitation to those with access to the knowledge

---

[27] Chambers, R. (1983/2014) *Rural development: Putting the last first*. New York: Routledge.

generated in the centers of research and study that Chambers calls "the core" has been to get closer both in their thoughts and emotions to the people they serve. We have tried through the educational materials that have been open to everyone from all walks of life to enhance their ability to judge the appropriateness and usefulness of research and study in programs related to development. We have called their attention to the unfortunate but undeniable fact that, during the past couple of decades, the conditions of life among the poor in the world's rural areas have drastically deteriorated. Why, we have asked, with all the resources available to us today, which include the capacity to study the problems faced by humanity, to discover their causes, and to overcome them systematically, are the efforts in the field of rural development failing so notably?

One can find a partial answer to this question in a debate between Robert Redfield, whose work has also shaped FUNDAEC's perspective on methodology, and the sociologist Oscar Lewis, which Richard Critchfield describes in his book *Villages*, published in 1983.[28] In 1926, Redfield, having lived in Tepoztlán, a village 50 miles south of Mexico City, provided a warm and sympathetic interpretation of life there. Seventeen years later, in 1943, Oscar Lewis visited the same village, presenting a contrasting view in his book, *"Tepoztlán Restudied,"* which critiqued Redfield's work. Lewis accused Redfield of presenting village life with a "Rousseauian quality" that downplayed evidence of violence, disruption, cruelty, poverty, disease, suffering, and maladjustment. While Redfield found Tepoztlán idyllic, Lewis described it as awful, marked by "fear, envy, and mistrust." In response, Redfield countered, alleging that Lewis lacked "humanity" and had imposed his "own values" on the village. During a talk in Sweden in 1953, Redfield noted that "personal interests and cultural values" inevitably influence anyone studying village life. He asserted that there were hidden questions behind both books about Tepoztlán. According to Redfield, the concealed question guiding his work was, "What do these people enjoy?" In contrast, he argued that the hidden question behind Dr. Lewis's book was, "What do these people suffer from?"

Bohm articulated that the inquiries we direct toward reality influence the responses we obtain. He contended that fragmented questions lead to fragmented answers. One of the implications of this idea for methodology, something that FUNDAEC has always had present in its work, is that scientists' concealed questions and implicit assumptions play a role in steering them to look for specific answers. Redfield's words resonate with the way Farzam expressed the essential questions that animated him and the first group of collaborators who took the initial steps that led to the creation of FUNDAEC.

---

[28] Critchfield, R. (1983) *Villages.* New York: Anchor Books.

Becoming acquainted with people as an agent of a development organization or bearer of charity is profoundly different from working among friends for a common purpose. In the latter case one's perceptions of reality are not shaped simply by academic theories that describe, from the outside, the needs and aspirations of the great masses of humanity. Although the gravity of social injustice is felt and understood, the integrity and the capacity for joy of its victims offers protection against some of the emotions that afflict external observers of poverty: pity, fear, sanctimonious indignation, ambivalence, and the inordinate desire to direct others to irrelevant paths laid out in accordance with one's own accomplishments or frustrations. For me, what was most striking about my new community was not material poverty per se but the wealth of talent that went uncultivated, together with the dreams of noble futures that were unfulfilled, as injustice systematically blocked the development of potentialities.[29]

This profound observation regarding the blocked potentialities of the population we engaged with ignited a steadfast commitment to nurture the inherent wealth of talents in the Norte del Cauca region and beyond. The enterprise that came to be identified as FUNDAEC, La Fundación para la Aplicación y Enseñanza de la Ciencia (the Foundation for the Application and Teaching of Science) aimed to pave the way for individuals to cultivate their abilities and for the collective aspiration of a dignified future to be realized. Spanning half a century, this mission and the practical steps we have taken to realize it have become a testament to the enduring hope that FUNDAEC will perpetually evolve and its champions will rise to meet this fundamental need. In this context, our continuous efforts seek not only to maintain but also to expand the fertile ground on which such dreams may thrive, ensuring that each generation has the opportunity to reach its potential and contribute meaningfully to the common good.

Weaving in Action: Groups and Learning Processes

We conclude this chapter by returning as a group (Haleh, Gustavo, and Bradley) to explain how FUNDAEC integrated these philosophical undercurrents introduced by Haleh into a pedagogical and methodological framework that seeks to close the theory-practice gap and actively engage in releasing human potentialities. Building on Haleh's earlier points, for FUNDAEC, recognizing the injustice of blocked human potentialities did not end with merely identifying this

---

[29] Arbab, F. (2000) 'Promoting a discourse on science, religion, and development' in Harper, S. (ed.) *The lab, the temple, and the market: Reflections at the intersection of science, religion, and development.* Canada: IDRC; Europe and the United States: Kumarian Press.

reality. Nor did it hold an empty optimism that sometime in the future, these potentialities would somehow become unblocked through the enlightened actions of others. Rather, for 50 years, FUNDAEC's champions have labored to develop an educational pedagogy and research methodology that enables groups in their communities and regions to read the social, environmental, spiritual, and economic text of their lived realities and take action to heal the relationships torn apart. Here, we take the weaving metaphor into its deeper logics, demonstrating how FUNDAEC's approach to development weaves the social fabric back together again through learning processes at the grassroots while overcoming the tendency or habit to allow divisiveness to block groups of collaborators from building more vibrant communities based on mutual assistance, cooperation, and trust.

FUNDAEC's educational processes have always sought to release human potentialities by fostering quality participation through establishing and forming groups in localities dedicated to a learning process in cycles of action-reflection, consultation, and study. Yet, working in groups is not such a simple practice and establishing a learning process based upon cycles of action-reflection, consultation, and study is not simple either; in combination, these two elements of FUNDAEC's approach avoid various pitfalls common to other approaches to development including individualism, ideological adherences, theory-practice gaps, and meaningless repetition of certain actions to prove the worth of a theory, method, diagnosis, model or

packaged solution. To clarify these concepts without an exhaustive discussion, we need to consider the elements of their structure. Drawing upon the metaphor of weaving on a loom, as we have used throughout the book, one could say that the structure that FUNDAEC, since the 1970s, created, practiced, and built is upon a warp and weft.

In weaving on a loom, the warp is the vertical strands of thread or yarn that remain stable and provide the firm architectural foundation on which one can construct various textiles. The weft is the horizontal strands of thread or yarn that get passed between the stable warp—traditionally by hand—methodically, in various patterns, giving the fabric its unique textures of color, feel, or consistency. The relationship between the warp and weft is the most essential feature of woven fabric. If they lack a firm and stable warp, the threads will begin to bunch and pull apart over time. Attentiveness to the weft—the unique qualities and characteristics of thread or yarn and the attributes, patterns, and colors in the desired fabric—can generate beautiful results. Below, we explain how groups of committed individuals work together in teams in a given place or region (the warp) and follow a patterned learning process composed of the elements of action-reflection, consultation, and study (the weft). Through these two related elements, FUNDAEC offers a distinctive and practical approach to development—the means for promoting community in diverse regions.

The warp in FUNDAEC's approach to development is the group, team, or nuclei of friends or coworkers who have prepared themselves—with the assistance of a tutor and texts—to orient their thoughts and practices toward mutual commitment, a dialogue of knowledges, modest projects, systematic observation, consultative decision-making, and service to the community. At the core of the group's purpose is the development of capabilities to promote community well-being across a range of concerns to the local population.

Throughout this book, we have dedicated considerable time to elaborating how FUNDAEC not only realized this essential element in the development of capabilities but also established programs (the SAT and the PSA) that have proven with great effect the long-term impacts of raising capabilities for integrated development for individuals, institutions and communities. It is not necessary to devote more time to describing all of the contents of the SAT and the PSA programs, the essential features of trained tutors who work with groups, nor the many and diverse projects that these groups of 10–15 people have advanced in communities from educating youth to health outreach, food production to environmental stewardship. Indeed, as previously indicated, to fully understand FUNDAEC's approach at a more intimate level, one would need to experience and be a dedicated member of such a group, immersing oneself in the learning process that unfolds.

The weft of FUNDAEC's approach to development is the learning process undertaken as the groups enter the field of development practice. The weft includes essential elements in a learning process: cycles of action, reflection, consultation, and study. Likened in some of FUNDAEC's texts as an orientation or "learning mode," these activities taking place in a given timeframe enable the groups engaged to examine and re-examine particular visions for change in a community, the strategies they may undertake to address a given problem in a region, and then to constantly return to these questions over and over again to modify future actions "as tasks are accomplished, obstacles removed, resources multiplied, and lessons learned."[30] Below, we elaborate more on each of these elements in greater detail.

Like weaving on a loom, a cycle of action-reflection flows through the warp—the group—in a period of active and purposeful movement in time. The learning process is not an end in itself; it is a means to an end—building more vibrant communities characterized by mutual assistance, cooperation, and trust. Action-reflection toward this end includes individuals and groups making observations while acknowledging patterns and synthesizing the features contributing to the whole or totality of possible disintegrative and integrative forces in their milieu. Rather than an overly cerebral exercise or highly ordered and fragmented method, action-reflection depends upon trusting oneself to intuitively experience but systematically record and analyze what one is experiencing as an individual and a group.

One way to describe action-reflection is the concept of attunement wherein someone grows in their ability to sense the social and environmental features they encounter and increase their responsiveness and resonance through time and practice. Farmers or gardeners, for instance, represent a social group of common experience who become attuned to the rhythms of nature and society through action-reflection over the cycles of the seasons. Therefore, time is an essential structuring element to action-reflection, and the concept of a cycle is critical to individual and collective practices in this methodology. Cycles provide those engaging in action-reflection an opportunity to constantly trace the change in their individual and collective understanding, assess the outcomes of certain actions, and renew their sense of purpose or commitment as an individual or group to a given goal or method. Most critically, a cycle provides entry and exit points for consultation.

Before moving on to consultation and its relationship to action-reflection cycles, FUNDAEC has always emphasized that action-reflection is not akin to the experimentation commonly associated with scientific inquiry into inanimate subjects or treating human subjects as

---

[30] Karlberg, M., & Correa, B. (2016). Development as systematic learning and capacity building. In *Education, Learning and the Transformation of Development* (pp. 19-35). Routledge.

objects of analysis. Building on the concept from Redfield about preserving our humanity and the humanity of the people within our communities, as well as Farzam's insistence that people in our communities be approached as friends when engaging in social endeavors, FUNDAEC held that it is crucial to refrain from treating human lives as variables in an experiment. For instance, teams prepared by FUNDAEC to engage in development do not create 'experimental' groups or schools. Instead, teams must commit wholeheartedly to educating with the best tools and knowledge available, never withholding benefits for research.

FUNDAEC encourages groups to thoughtfully take action to benefit the community, utilizing all available resources to achieve a specific goal. However, societal transformation is a gradual journey. Groups must take measured steps, constantly reflecting on progress. With each action, they must ask: What have we achieved in a given project? How can this be the foundation for more significant progress that extends further or makes necessary adjustments? Do we have increased knowledge or resources to take a more considerable step? These questions can guide more deliberate lines of action in the next phase. Thus, action and reflective practice form the core of FUNDAEC's systematic learning process. It is a cycle of doing, learning from doing, and then doing better; we strive to transform society as participants, not observers.

Consultation is an essential element in the establishment of a learning process. Through genuine consultation, FUNDAEC recognized that the pursuit of truth transcends the customary approaches of negotiation and compromise found in today's discussions on human matters. In its purest form, consultation is a dialogue of knowledges that seeks unity and serves the common good. Such a high standard of truth-seeking is incompatible with the culture of contention, antagonism, and relentless criticism prevalent in modern society. Methods of control, domination, marginalization, debate, partisanship, and adversarial tactics are detrimental to the essence of a dialogue of knowledges necessary for consultation. The goal of consultation is not a negative compromise but rather to reach a positive consensus on the truth and make the best possible decision from the available knowledge in the group at any moment. Consultation does not need to happen at just one point in time. Indeed, one can always return to consultation should new information emerge, capabilities develop, and obstacles or opportunities arise. When combined with action-reflection, groups can advance in their understanding and sustain a continuous growth process in understanding and action.

Yet, more than just a mechanism for reflecting as a group or decision-making, FUNDAEC's understanding of consultation has a moral quality; it involves individuals who participate and strive to go beyond their own perspectives to act as members of a unified body with collective interests and goals. Consultation implies folding our interests into a collective and, in doing so, being reminded of our responsibilities to a broader process of promoting community well-being, not merely proving a point or feeling satisfied with one's accumulated knowledge, personal experience, or point of view. In an environment where we balance openness with respect, we share ideas collectively—not owned by the person who suggests them during the discussion. They can be accepted, discarded, or modified to further the group's objectives. We measure the success of the consultation by the degree to which all participants support the conclusions reached, irrespective of their initial personal views. We are open to revising a decision if subsequent experiences reveal flaws, reflecting collective decision-making's dynamic and progressive nature.

The final element of FUNDAEC's approach to establishing a learning process is study and the systematization and dissemination of knowledge. FUNDAEC distinguishes between these two practices as they represent different steps in a learning process. We begin with the concept of study. Complementing cycles of action-reflection with consultation and study, individually and collectively, provides us with access to knowledge which has been generated and applied in other places, insights gleaned through systematic observation, and concepts that could be useful in multiple contexts and which can enhance the quality of ideas discussed in a given consultation. FUNDAEC would acknowledge that study alone is insufficient to bring about the great changes necessary in communities. Likewise, cycles of action-reflection without study may fail to draw upon important insights from elsewhere; consultation may never advance based on new insights, getting stuck in repetition and the limits of the group's experience. Study, like action-reflection and consultation, require dedication at the individual and collective level. Individual initiative to study available sources of knowledge and information among each collective member is vital to action-reflection and consultation. It is not sufficient that only one individual should dedicate themselves to studying beyond the scope of a given area; all must make an effort to enhance collective inquiry and the learning process.

The second aspect of study concerns the systematization and dissemination of knowledge. For every action-reflection cycle, teams apply the most appropriate and rigorous methods for recording observations, gathering information, collecting data, analyzing results, or presenting our findings in that field of inquiry. Generating knowledge nourishes our ability to learn and to study. Should not this knowledge and experience be shared for the benefit of all? Knowledge sharing necessitates systematic efforts that document learning and provide a means for the elaboration of future educational texts or the application of new knowledge or concepts in the development field in another region.

Yet, for FUNDAEC, documentation and dissemination are not ends in themselves; they are not detached from our present actions, future actions, or the potential actions of others in other places. Studies must serve those directly involved in the actions of which the teams dedicated to systematizing learning are also a part. In that sense, FUNDAEC eschews lengthy studies that delay action or justify inaction. FUNDAEC believes in a dynamic balance between the results communicated and the actions taken, where each informs and enhances the other. Studies, in sum, are also an essential feature of the learning process, which systematizes experiences from cycles of action-reflection and nourishes consultation.

We wish to conclude our discussion of the warp and weft of FUNDAEC's approach by drawing attention to the most vital aspects of weaving a fabric of unity, without which all this talk and conceptualization would lack meaning and purpose: the weavers and the thread. FUNDAEC's approach holds that releasing human potentialities depends upon agents of change—the people or weavers—and the unique and distinctive environments and conditions in the regions where they live—the thread. Conscious of the disintegrative forces at work in society and their effects on the essential relationships binding people and the environment, FUNDAEC still recognizes the creativity and artistry that every human being possesses, which can enable them to assist others in seeing the world as a whole and to heal the breach in the threads and make their unique contribution to the well-being of their communities.

Furthermore, FUNDAEC has always, from the beginning, seen that central to learning processes is a profound respect and honor for the natural environment upon which humanity depends to thrive—the material thread that binds us all together, planet Earth. One cannot underestimate—given the divides that we confront today—the extent to which groups and learning processes must catalyze and raise the spirits of a new generation of weavers; ones capable of appreciating, caring for, and repairing the threads which have been broken, and creating fabrics anew based on establishing groups mutually committed to cycles of action-reflection, consultation and study in every locality, in every region of the world. Yet, first, we must pick up the threads and begin weaving, conscious of our high purpose and cognizant of a distinctive approach to development which may, in the decades ahead, enable our communities to reach higher levels of spiritual and material well-being. However, this work will not be easy, and we must consider it more deeply, learn its subtleties, and gain greater experience through individual and collective practice with its warp and weft.

Picking Up the Threads

As gardens began to appear in the community, everyone
wanted to be part of this nascent movement, replicating what
others were doing. Many became aware of the abundant spaces
around their homes that they could utilize. Others realized
they could form partnerships with landowners, and some even
reclaimed spaces belonging to the municipality for use. This
participation in food production injected new life into
interpersonal relationships, as people felt they were part of a
far-reaching collective effort.

Gustavo Correa

Opening

In the previous chapter, Releasing Human Potentialities, we attempted to provide conceptual insight into FUNDAEC's distinctive approach to development, including the warp and weft of its weaving. As we described, FUNDAEC prepares individuals and groups to make a mutual commitment—to promote the well-being of their communities—and invites them to participate in a learning process, which includes cycles of action-reflection, consultation, and study. This cycle trains them to create a collective vision and strategies for change while defining their activities and modifying future actions as they complete tasks, overcome obstacles, grow resources, and acquire new knowledge related to the initiatives they undertake.

We call this chapter "Picking Up the Threads" to highlight the active weaving work of FUNDAEC in Colombia and worldwide to address the challenges facing the communities in which its programs operate. Our final chapter attempts to demonstrate FUNDAEC's approach in practice, where groups working together in cycles of action-reflection, consultation, and study seek to promote regenerative agriculture in Norte del Cauca. The Growing Hope project draws on the immense potential for food system transformation set in motion from the capacities built through FUNDAEC's Sistema de Aprendizaje Tutorial (SAT) and Preparation for Social Action (PSA) Programs, its deep networks and relationships in four communities, its demonstration farm in Perico Negro, and its connections to K–11 schools in the region of Norte del Cauca.

This conversation includes Ever Rivera and Maria Cristina Mosquera, coordinators of different aspects of the project in Norte del Cauca whose leadership provides a critical perspective on the unfolding of activities and receptivity of the population to participation. As the reader progresses through the chapter, we hope they notice the recurring themes from earlier in the book, such as a dialogue of knowledges, trust, long-term commitments, building capabilities, participation, the essential wholeness of nature and society, and the attitudes necessary for community engagement.

Through our conversation, we not only want to emphasize the importance of groups and the learning process, but we also hope the project's story serves as a call and encouragement to others to take up this kind of work in their own contexts and learn the nuances of the approach taken. We hope this chapter inspires our readers to consider—amidst a time of crisis—what is possible if we steadily cultivate capacities through time and how intergenerational dialogue, the formation of committed groups, and the initiation of cycles of action-reflection, consultation, and study can advance real transformation at the community and regional level—starting in a particular place.

As we have traced throughout the conversation thus far, the organic growth of FUNDAEC's work has paralleled a dedicated commitment to the development and well-being of people, communities, and the region of the place of its birth. While actors in the fields of education and development worldwide recognize FUNDAEC's work—its pioneering tutorial learning model, its focus on generating and applying knowledge, its building of capacities, as well as the hundreds of thousands of participants in both the SAT and the PSA programs—our final chapter attempts to illustrate FUNDAEC's approach to development by looking closely at a project initiated by FUNDAEC within the past three years. Growing Hope harnesses the human potential and existing capacity of historic collaborators with FUNDAEC in the Norte del Cauca region, including hundreds of its graduates and members of grassroots organizations over the past 50 years. Responding to the food crisis caused by the pandemic, FUNDAEC sprung into action, working closely with groups of small-scale producers, rural educators, and youth development specialists to consolidate their efforts toward food sovereignty through regenerative agriculture in Norte del Cauca.

Central to FUNDAEC's vision is the role of small-scale farmers and home gardeners. Since its inception in the 1970s, FUNDAEC has collaborated with these groups to develop research in agricultural production systems, following principles similar to those recognized today as regenerative agriculture. Its dedication to agro-ecological methods and regenerative agriculture, a hallmark of FUNDAEC's programming, has meant that many people across Norte del Cauca, Colombia, and beyond have learned these approaches from their programs. This amounts to hundreds of thousands of individuals capable of producing food and possessing the basic knowledge to rebuild food systems from the ground up. Highly diversified but efficient crop parcels are one of the production models developed. These lots are between 500 and 1,000 square meters of short-cycle associated crops, which use preferably native seeds, are fertilized by organic fertilizer, use live covers and staggered sowing, and are delimited with live fences. Another recently developed model focuses on agroforestry, interspersing fruit, and timber trees in larger extensions with transitory crops.

FUNDAEC's Growing Hope project was not a spontaneous outburst of activity responding to a new fad or movement. In the introduction of the book, Gustavo Correa introduced the emergence of FUNDAEC in parallel with the devastating effects of the Green Revolution, a vision for global agriculture and food system development that would—over 50 years—fundamentally transform people's everyday lives, transform soils, forests, climate, and traditional farming systems, transform the global food supply, and provoke a demographic transition from rural to urban areas that moved billions of people from livelihoods tied to land stewardship to lives in search of labor opportunities. Every human being on earth has been touched—unequally—by this revolution in agriculture, food production, distribution, consumption, and its attendant shifts in the social and environmental landscape. As Gustavo described, in the 1970s and the decades to follow, movements composed of peasants, farmers, farm workers, laborers, and consumers would question, contest, and challenge the imposition of these economic models, agricultural techniques, food products, and market systems in their regions and pursue alternative paths and visions of development.

As we have learned, FUNDAEC—with its vision, approach, and development practice—took shape in a specific region impacted by Green Revolution technologies and the consolidation of the sugarcane industry. Sugar has not only transformed the environmental landscape of Norte del Cauca, but its consumption has also become one of the leading causes of diet-related disease, and its production is a key contributor to ongoing carbon emissions and anthropogenic climate change. When one thinks of the need for a change in the global food system, the sugar industry and its impacted communities, like Norte del Cauca, are vital places to begin. However, one of the key challenges today is that the destiny of sugarcane production in Colombia is no longer the same as in the past. Sugarcane is one of the leading biofuels promoted in Colombia and globally as a replacement for fossil fuels. In the past decade, demand for ethanol through the sugarcane agro-industry has continued to accelerate agricultural change, exacerbating food system vulnerabilities and causing further social and environmental landscape degradation.

Sugarcane now constitutes 88.5% of the permanent crops in this region. Many recognize sugarcane for its intensive use of agrochemicals and heavy machinery, the deskilling and displacement of local communities, its threat to the native flora and fauna, extreme pressure on land, labor, and water resources, and its large carbon footprint due to burning fields, fossil fuel inputs, and growing adoption for biofuels in-vehicle use. Demand for sugarcane production has increased property concentration, with 5% of the population owning more than 60% of the land. This inequitable distribution of productive land in Norte del Cauca threatens its inhabitants' food self-sufficiency and negatively influences their perceptions and practices related to family and community life. As a result, increased social conflict, hopelessness, and despair in Norte del Cauca parallels declining community food security in the region. These social realities are central to the place-based and regional context of the work of FUNDAEC. In addition to its systematic observation and acute and deeply empathetic and embedded understanding of agrarian change and its impacts on the livelihoods of the people in Norte del Cauca over the past 50 years, FUNDAEC also drew, intentionally and exhaustively, from various sources of knowledge—scientific and spiritual—that guided its efforts and sustained its protagonists and participants through these decades.

As we learn below, FUNDAEC's Growing Hope project took shape in response to the food shortages caused by the global pandemic. However, its capacity to respond and the quality of community participation in its networks was not an accidental or spontaneous occurrence. Growing Hope might be likened to a demonstration project that closes the first 50-year cycle of FUNDAEC's work and opens a new cycle of growth. First launched by a group initiating a cycle of action-reflection, consultation, and study focused on small-scale farmers and agro-ecological practice in 1974, now in 2024, FUNDAEC is still pressing forward; its countless graduates and practitioners are laboring to advance the agro-ecological and regenerative agricultural practices that these action research teams rediscovered among Afro-Colombian and indigenous communities in Norte del Cauca and have promoted ever since. Today, they are redoubling their efforts to raise the human resources necessary to transform the regional food system in Norte del Cauca.

This conversation offers a glimpse into that effort. The conversation will begin with Gustavo telling the project's history, followed by reflections on the project's growth from the standpoints of Haleh and Bradley, as well as Ever Rivera and María Cristina Mosquera, key leaders in the initiatives underway.

Bradley

In the past three years, FUNDAEC has embarked on various ambitious projects in communities across Colombia. Gustavo, you have referred to this as a flourishing activity coinciding with FUNDAEC's 50th anniversary. What do you mean by this idea of flourishing, and how did these projects come about? What has contributed to the flourishing of environmental, agricultural, and community food projects in FUNDAEC over the past few years? What was the stimulus, so to speak, from your perspective?

Gustavo

In 2019, the pandemic thrust the world in an unprecedented global crisis. With its unexpected onset, it profoundly disrupted a period of relative tranquility in FUNDAEC's work. Faced with the pandemic's far-reaching effects—which shook the foundations of the social and economic order—FUNDAEC navigated uncharted waters. The imperative to persist in alleviating the stark realities of the emergency, especially within the communities we had long partnered with, was unmistakable. Through thoughtful deliberation, we examined the shortcomings of economic models that now profoundly affect those we serve. Acknowledging that the challenge of devising viable solutions was beyond our capacities, we endeavored to contribute our part, building on groundwork established over decades. This effort included leveraging community and individual capabilities to undertake collective projects, deploy agricultural technologies and production systems, and reinforce the cohesive social fabric strengthened by enduring bonds of affection, fellowship, and deep respect for knowledge.

At the onset of the pandemic in Colombia, around 700 students were actively participating in the PSA program alongside 800 graduates, which included 120 trained tutors recognized as genuine leaders and advocates for community well-being. Despite the challenges, 70 tutors led groups of 10–15 students and helped recruit new groups. They played a pivotal role in raising community awareness regarding the critical situation the pandemic presented and the necessary measures to protect the health of children and adults. Simultaneously, they seized this opportunity to foster dialogue on the need to collectively address families' escalating economic struggles. The food shortage was the catalyst that spurred everyone into immediate action.

The interest sparked by the initial conversations about food production among the PSA program participants, past graduates, and their families, neighbors, and coworkers gave us renewed encouragement. It also confirmed the potential for action within the network of tutors and students, all of whom were confronting the same pervasive crisis. Living in agricultural regions had not insulated people from the impact; they were just as dependent on market systems for their food as urban consumers. With the expertise we've developed over the years and the agricultural component of the PSA program as a foundation, we saw an opportunity for a strategic emphasis. It became imperative to use our collectively accumulated knowledge and refocus our energies on enhancing food production capabilities within these communities. Our immediate task was to reinforce our constant efforts to transform rural residents from dependent consumers to self-sufficient producers, equipping them with the tools to resist and thrive amid adversity.

Through our deliberations, we concluded that the time was ripe to work together to boost food production using the network of participants as the catalyst. Local groups were already in place, and unit and regional coordinators, along with our national coordinating teams, began to consult, study, and initiate cycles of action-reflection focused on food production. Below are excerpts from dialogues during some of the consultations that took place among these teams and across the networks as a whole, captured in recorded discussions among PSA tutors and FUNDAEC staff.

We are receiving feedback from the PSA program's students and tutors indicating that they struggle to obtain food. This challenge stems from restrictions on movement and heavy reliance on local markets' supplies of regional imports, including products with the

PSA students and tutors, department of Córdoba

potential for local cultivation. Some PSA students who have land are advocating for and initiating an increase in local food production and a community-based exchange of produce to address this state of emergency. I believe that FUNDAEC should initiate actions to bolster these local initiatives.

The pandemic has laid bare the fragility of the global food distribution system, which concentrates production in a few hubs, often far from consumers. Globally, many countries, even those well-suited for agriculture, have dangerously increased their reliance on these production centers. Urbanization has distanced people from the land and diminished the widespread knowledge of food production, which is critical for human survival. I can assure you that many children in urban schools have never seen a tomato plant or an eggplant in person.

This detachment from the land and the shifting away from food production isn't confined to urban areas. I've observed people no longer planting trees or cornstalk in rural towns. The fruits they harvest come from trees planted by their grandparents. This trend is more prevalent among the youth, who—due to a lack of opportunities—are waiting for a chance to migrate elsewhere. That's why the elderly and more conscientious individuals deeply value conversations with PSA students, as it rekindles hope within them.

One thing that this collective effort to produce food shows is the use of all the available labor within the family. In these gardens, not only the most skilled in agricultural tasks collaborate but also every family member: the grandparents, the children, or even those with some physical limitations. And not to mention the

Community action, Siloé neighborhood, Cali, Valle, 2020

satisfaction of sitting down at the table to eat what they have sown with so much effort.

We have noticed a change in participation and the quality of conversations. Everywhere, you hear discussions about how to prepare and improve the soil, how to fertilize, how to control insects, what to plant and produce, how to improve the soil, and what the vegetative period of a plant is. Since there are more questions than answers, an interest in researching and learning more has arisen.

Working with the earth is contagious. Seeing others happy, focused, and content in their work draws many people in. It seems to me that it slows people's pace, bringing calm and tranquility. Many who before saw the work as isolated and burdensome have joined efforts with others and see that not only is their work better rewarded, but also that they strengthen friendships, enjoy the company of others, and form a community.

I see the product exchange as an interesting scheme for distributing production. Not everyone can produce everything, so everyone is willing to exchange monetary or otherwise with what they have. I have also noticed a sense of solidarity, generosity, and fair trade awakening. I consider this to be the basis of a peasant economy.

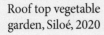

Roof top vegetable
garden, Siloé, 2020

Not everything happened in rural areas. The city of Cali also felt the impact of the effort to produce food. Yesterday, the office's neighbors came to ask if the products coming out of the garden were for sale. Before, they would pass by without paying much attention. Given the difficulty of acquiring food, people's curiosity is now piqued, and everyone wants to know how to produce food in their home gardens…

We must acknowledge that farming requires substantial effort. It's incredibly challenging to persevere without passion and a love for the land. That's why I believe the agricultural component of the PSA program should make room to explore various technologies to make the work easier and more efficient. We must investigate cutting-edge yet appropriate technologies for small-scale farms to ensure cost isn't a barrier to their adoption.

I would like to address land access. In many regions where we work, rural dwellers have been relegated to less fertile land and, over time, reduced to small plots that diminish their hope for food self-sufficiency. There are numerous movements advocating for genuine land reform as the solution. One could join them, but continuing on the path we've charted is better. On this path, we must identify the comparative advantages of small-scale production and build a robust local economy. If land reform does come, we'll be better prepared to avoid repeating the cycle of

Vegetable garden
at FUNDAEC's
Cali Office, 2023

owning land, not knowing how to make it productive, and eventually losing it.

I thought we had lost the fight against large-scale production that relies on the technological packages of the Green Revolution, dependent on agrochemicals and improved seeds. However, the pandemic shows us that we must reconsider this path to feeding the world's population—not just because of the food distribution system but also due to health problems and malnutrition resulting from consuming products laden with toxic residues and produced on increasingly biologically degraded soils. Production closer to consumption centers, involving everyone as producers on living soils regenerating themselves, will offer better protection in global events like the pandemic.

What you've just mentioned reminds me of our last meeting with the farmers of Perico Negro, who, to our satisfaction, attended in greater numbers than expected. The general sentiment was that their land was becoming less productive, that to grow anything, they had to increase chemical fertilization, and that pests had become more prevalent. They also suffer from the insensitivity of middlemen who overlook the rising production costs on increasingly impoverished soil. They trust in FUNDAEC's efforts to promote healthier, environmentally friendly agriculture. These comments and the effects of the pandemic indicate that it's time to be bolder in promoting what we've learned over the years and to convince ourselves that we haven't lost the fight. On the contrary, the environment is ripe for the ideas of agroecology, sustainable agriculture, and all the terms in use today to flourish.

Regional gathering of farmers at FUNDAEC's University Center,
Perico Negro, 2023

Food production projects of PSA students and tutors,
various regions of Colombia, 2020

Comments like the above were heard daily, increasing enthusiasm and urgency to take action.

FUNDAEC initiated a series of online workshops led by PSA tutors, with the participation of their students and other community members. These workshops emphasized the need to produce food for both family consumption and the local market and reviewed the processes for establishing productive projects adapted to individual conditions. Additionally, the steps to establish a family garden were detailed. Enthusiasm for this effort grew as participants shared their progress and experiences. By the end of 2020, after just a few months of activity, around 859 gardens and another 139 productive projects of different natures had been established. However, gardens and food production were not the only outcomes observed in this cycle of action and reflection.

As gardens began to appear in the community, everyone wanted to be part of this nascent movement, replicating what others were doing. Many became aware of the abundant spaces around their homes that they could utilize. Others realized they could form partnerships with landowners, and some even reclaimed spaces belonging to the municipality for use. This participation in food production injected new life into interpersonal relationships, as people felt they were part of a far-reaching collective effort. And when harvest time came, the bonds of friendship tightened further, enabling the exchange of produce and making food more accessible to those who, due to health, age, or other reasons, couldn't join the physical labor. It was heartening to witness the generosity of individuals, the joy of sharing the fruits of their labor with others, the depth of conversations that ensued, and the collective desire to continue working together.

What was described above did not consist of loose conversations or disconnected and disorganized activities; rather, it reflected the distinctive approach FUNDAEC has been practicing for decades. There is deep but not prolonged dialogue, possibilities are identified based on what has been built, conscientious enthusiasm is generated, and a coherent action plan with a high chance of success is defined. We have always been aware that community processes become more sustainable when we choose to implement a simple action plan in clear stages, with well-focused actions and visible, measurable short-term results. This is preferable to a very elaborate plan that takes a long time to show its benefits and whose actions tend to disperse easily. In our conception of learning, engaging in broad, continuous, and sincere conversations with all participants during the implementation of any project, conducted with a research-oriented attitude, allows us to better assimilate both successes and failures.

The success experienced by everyone in this food production initiative demonstrated the execution power of the network of participants in FUNDAEC's programs. This network, activated through virtual media, opened countless possibilities for us to coordinate and support development processes in several distant communities in Colombia more efficiently. We could now establish more intimate relationships with different actors and closely monitor activities. Participants were united around a common purpose, roles, and responsibilities were clearly defined, and conflict-free relationships flourished. The moment seemed propitious to add another element to what was becoming a larger project.

Reflecting on the effects of the pandemic, some of our conversations revolved around the alarming disparities that had always existed but were now becoming more evident. These disparities highlighted the difference between those who have the means to comfortably confront an emergency and those in a position of high and permanent vulnerability. We discussed equally devastating situations that could be exacerbated by the effects of global warming, affecting everyone, but where the most vulnerable will again bear the brunt. We also listened to voices warning us about the connection between the emergence of future pandemics and the depletion of nature's resources.

Given that FUNDAEC's programs do not operate in isolation but are influenced by their surroundings, we could not ignore this reality. We felt that, in addition to food security, we needed to address environmental issues more specifically, not only in speech but also in action. To this end, we once again utilized our network of participants. We designed a campaign to plant 10,000 trees in the environments of the network members. To ensure this did not remain a temporary effort, the PSA program incorporated environmental activity as one of its permanent components.

We know that planting trees is a small action and not "the solution" to the enormous problem of global warming. However, we also understand that big problems are not always solved with great solutions. Often, small, continuous, interconnected, locally designed, and controlled actions can have unpredictable effects of great impact. This new undertaking was not merely about emphasizing certain topics in the PSA curriculum or adding new practices. Rather, it was seen as a way to give new impetus to the development process in each locality and to enliven individual and collective commitment in the hearts and minds of all program participants, who would extend this commitment to their families and other community members.

Just as establishing community family gardens had a profound impact, planting trees and restoring the beauty of the landscape was expected to deeply affect people's hearts and interpersonal relationships. Harmonious contact with nature is a powerful motivating force that brings out human traits of solidarity, generosity, wonder, and appreciation for beauty. It awakens the need for connection and ignites the thirst for knowledge in the face of the vast biological world, its myriad relationships and exchanges, and the secrets it holds. Reflecting on and contemplating the beauty and perfection of nature inspires the construction of peaceful and harmonious relationships and soothes the persistent forces that separate and isolate.

As a result of consultations among participants, we committed to planting 10,000 trees, primarily fruit trees but also timber and forage trees. The campaign significantly impacted community awareness and learning. Many were motivated to learn about native trees, identify endangered species, and understand their use and care. Workshops were designed and implemented for the construction and operation of local nurseries. Entire families and students from primary and secondary schools attended the festive planting days, participating and generating new initiatives. Interactions with various community actors highlighted the need to engage the region's formal educational institutions to create spaces for reflection on environmental degradation and to generate similar projects as part of their regular activities. These activities were made possible with financial support from the Two Wings Foundation in Austria and the Mona Foundation in the United States.

Our colleague Emilio Constantino, who provided technical assistance to the project, shared with us an interesting perspective on other tree-planting campaigns in which he has participated:

> Our original goal was to plant 10,000 trees. Our agroforestry team has experience with large planting campaigns; we recently planted 600,000 trees in one region for a company. The problem we see globally with planting millions of trees is that they don't reach maturity. There are big goals, and planting can happen, but nobody accompanies the trees. The projects mobilize people to plant them, but nothing is heard from them again. After two or three years, almost no trees survive these large-scale planting projects.

> But, when we approached this modest project with FUNDAEC to plant 10,000 trees and visited the communities across the country, the agroforestry team immediately realized that this was a very different project, with much more potential for success than we have ever seen. For the first time I can remember, our team had total certainty that we would obtain good results because of the ethics and commitment of the people. The youth from the participating PSA programs stood out above any project I have ever seen. These people's commitment to sponsoring tree planting has been incredible. Their commitment goes beyond planting them—accompanying the trees until they mature.

PSA students and tutors planting native trees and establishing a nursery, department of Córdoba

However, in the communities collaborating with FUNDAEC, we have seen this great potential for the trees to reach maturity. We believe the project is developing a new religion of nature conservation among the youth, a religion of conservation, stewardship, and tree planting. We are very grateful that FUNDAEC invited us to participate in their project. We are very excited by the potential unleashed from it. We see the possibility of establishing relationships with friends and commitments in the long term, which is very important to us as an agroforestry team. We want to ensure that communities understand and take ownership of the importance of trees in their environment. FUNDAEC and the PSA program are enabling that to happen. In a sense, we can now achieve these goals for the first time.

As the tree-planting campaign progressed and generated new knowledge and understanding, our studies intensified, and our conversations broadened and deepened. The discourse describing the development strategy of the region evolved and was enriched by this new element. Continuous references to the rural landscape fostered closeness and gratitude, becoming an effective, practical, and appreciated way for everyone to integrate the emphasis on protecting and caring for our "shared home" and food security into daily conversations. We discussed how the markers of development progress in a region include the adoption of a discourse that reflects the inhabitants' awareness of food security, the urgency of protecting and intelligently using natural resources ("divine gifts" as they were called before), and the beautification of the landscape through diverse agricultural and livestock production, varied flora and fauna, the presence of forests, and proper water management.

In this post-pandemic environment, and given the results of the initiatives carried out by participants of the FUNDAEC programs in different regions of Colombia, we felt it was an opportune time to advance research within the agricultural and livestock production process. This process had been weakened to meet the demands of various organizations implementing the PSA in different places. The principles contained in the emerging discourse of regenerative agriculture at the farmers' level harmonized well with those that had guided FUNDAEC's agricultural and livestock research.

Insightful discussions with Roy Steiner from the Rockefeller Foundation, who visited us during that time, highlighted other aspects that we also had to consider: the critical roles of food forests, enhanced child nutrition in schools, and the urgent need to support small producers in adapting to climate change. These discussions, coupled with the support from the Wayfarer Foundation, Mona Foundation, and Two Wings Foundation, underscored the significance of our collective endeavor. The unwavering backing from the Bahá'í International Development Organization for raising community development promoters, alongside a fertile environment for collaborative innovation in regenerative agriculture, underscored the moment's fortuitous alignment. This combination of support and shared vision prompted us to concentrate our efforts in the region of our inception, Norte del Cauca, as we embark on a new cycle of FUNDAEC's existence. Here, we aimed to weave a narrative of progress, resilience, and community harmony rooted in the land that first inspired us.

We articulated our renewed vision as transitioning individual producers and communities towards regenerative agriculture. Realizing this vision involved more decisively discontinuing conventional farming practices and making room for those that enhance diversity, using organic fertilizers, eliminating soil plowing, utilizing locally produced native seeds, and introducing advanced technologies suitable for making manual labor more efficient. It also meant focusing production on local consumption and promoting local markets to bridge the gap between producers and consumers. To solidify the transformation that would occur, the goals, activities, achievements, and learnings should be widely disseminated among all levels of the community, especially schools and colleges and the numerous grassroots organizations. Within this framework of regenerative agriculture, the Growing Hope project was

Solidarity groups
meeting together,
Norte del Cauca,
1990s

Solidarity groups
working together,
Norte del Cauca,
1990s

Village store in La Dominga, Norte del Cauca, 1990s

FUNDAEC's Agro-industrial Center in La Arrobleda, 1990s

Transforming primary production, Agro-industrial Center, La Arrobleda, 1990s

FUNDAEC's Integral Farm for Regenerative Agriculture, Perico Negro, 2024

conceived to support groups of farmers from four communities through their transition process. This project, building upon nearly three years of effort, took shape around a core team and many collaborators who have dedicated themselves to advancing across a range of project elements.

The results of research conducted years ago on various rural life processes have provided a foundation for new knowledge. As previously mentioned, one way these results are disseminated is through the texts used in FUNDAEC programs, which are periodically improved and updated. At a recent gathering, a farmer's insight transported us back to several FUNDAEC initiatives from the 1990s focused on diversified models of small-scale farming and solidarity-based models of production and economic cooperation. He conveyed with conviction that our working together was not something new but was actually "intensifying our journey towards regenerative agriculture through a seamless continuation of a well-established path."

The Food Forest, with the Bahá'í House of Worship of Norte del Cauca in the distance

Transitioning to regenerative agriculture, in our experience, requires conviction, faith, training, collective effort, and financial support to supplement one's income during the transition period. Restoring the soil to full biological life is a process that necessitates constant inquiry, detailed knowledge of each space and its surroundings, and an intense exchange of information and experiences. Although it is a slow process, it offers great economic and emotional rewards in the medium and long term: the potential to produce healthier food, increase soil productivity, ensure a constant supply of nutritious food on families' tables, and provide full employment for the family workforce.

Nursery at the Food Forest   Planting trees in the Food Forest

Even now, in this short amount of time, the effects of this transition are becoming evident in several key areas: the innovative practices adopted by farmers, the strengthened bonds between participants, the enriched and broadened discourse in conversations, and the emergence of a varied landscape that challenges the dominance of monoculture and revitalizes different environments. The cohesive force of regenerative agriculture's practices and principles is reinvigorating community initiatives aimed at the common good and energizing the local economy's dynamics. As this rejuvenated approach to food production progresses, distinctive elements of a comprehensive rural development strategy materialize.

The landscape of Norte del Cauca has been enriched with various developments, notably the 'Integral Farm for Regenerative Agriculture' at the FUNDAEC facilities in Perico Negro. This farm includes training and lodging spaces, cultivated sectors for demonstrating the principles of regenerative agriculture, and several business units managed by community groups for producing organic fertilizers and native seeds. Additionally, a 10-hectare mother forest has been established in the town of Agua Azul, with nearly 1,400 native fruit trees, timber, and forage species. The hope is that other forests, beautifying different communities and inspiring further collective projects, will emerge from this initiative.

These early results are encouraging. Central to this transition process is the role of a promoter of community wellbeing, who acts as a catalyst for collective efforts, a transmitter of evolving knowledge, and a resource for training. We hope that once the transition process in the four communities of Norte del Cauca—Perico Negro, Agua Azul, Puerto Tejada, and Alegrías—is sufficiently advanced, and the necessary management capacity and resources are available, we will be able to expand the scope of the project.

PSA students planting native trees in Bolívar, Córdoba, 2022

The Growing Hope project injects new vitality into FUNDAEC by creating a regional learning and development center. Its mission is to nurture groups of farmers and promoters dedicated to the community's wellbeing, united in their noble aspirations and prepared to drive the transformations needed in various environments. These individuals, embedded in their communities, are inspired by a deep sense of service and equipped with the expertise necessary to promote and sustain community advancement.

At the center of our efforts is the integration of spiritual and scientific knowledge, which, along with the knowledge generated through action, combines the complementary aspects of a comprehensive development strategy. This provides individuals and communities with the means for active participation. By enriching the knowledge base, we bring together efforts to elevate local farmers' agricultural practices and distribution networks, thereby promoting ecological stewardship, social harmony, and economic progress. This meticulously crafted, integrative approach strengthens the fabric of the community and lays a solid foundation for lasting peace.

We are convinced that every social project undertaken in Colombia, a country marked by age-long and persistent violence, must have a healing effect and promote justice and unity: the unity of people, strategies, resources, and wills. Achieving peace is a collective aspiration, and numerous approaches have attempted to cultivate it. In our case, we have witnessed the transformations in people involved in FUNDAEC's initiatives after the pandemic. These activities foster life, create closeness, and establish deep connections between participants, dispelling the shadows of violence. We are convinced that true peace begins with a transformation of the heart.

Finally, I would like to add that the constant reference to concepts exploring the relationships in nature within FUNDAEC materials significantly amplifies this effect. The ever-observable symbiosis in nature enhances and strengthens attempts to build human relationships inspired by the principles of cooperation, reciprocity, and mutual aid. This perspective opens a new dimension to the project, revealing that regenerative agriculture transcends its primary function. It emerges as a powerful catalyst for peace within communities and offers a ray of hope. By caring for the land, we foster peace among its people, illustrating that planting trees, cultivating the soil, and establishing gardens are a safe investment in achieving community harmony and hope for a peaceful future.

Maria Cristina Mosquera

Today, through the Growing Hope project, we are redoubling our efforts and recommitting ourselves to working with Norte Caucano farmers, schools, and communities. The SAT and the PSA programs focus on agriculture and emphasize developing the youth's capacities to plant diversified plots and create home gardens that support household and community food security. Thousands of students currently enrolled in our programs in Colombia are focused on this area and practicing this in their communities. Starting in late 2021, we began focusing on this very closely, looking at agricultural production and the role of gardens in food sovereignty. We are rediscovering all the processes that are taking place there in the farming communities. This work started with an exploratory phase of talking to farmers, visiting the plots, and investigating a little. We began asking: how are the farmers doing, and how are they arranging their plots today?

We are finding more problems today than in the 1970s and 1980s. The farmers say the soil is no longer fertile, and their plots are not producing as they once did. We have visited homes and farms, observing their production techniques, the relationships between farmers, and the marketing processes of their products. We have had several conversations with farmers who have gladly accepted. They have great confidence in FUNDAEC and great hopes for the results of our joint work on their plots. They feel that they are part of the action-research process to transform agriculture in the region. I believe that these farmers and family members gladly accepted this invitation because they recognized FUNDAEC's commitment to the region. Some pointed out that FUNDAEC had been there for a long time, but they had not taken advantage of it enough. That is why now they want to reconnect with FUNDAEC and benefit from all the experience.

In initial conversations with long-time acquaintances and others who joined them, we noted a sincere interest in learning more about the principles of regenerative agriculture and the social philosophy that underpins it. They also showed great interest in participating in the trials we proposed to gather information for developing a production model based on these principles. This model would be adapted to specific conditions such as soil structure, climate, property history, and fertility level. They expressed the urgency of finding practices that restore the fertility of their soils and their productivity. In subsequent conversations, the issue of the market, small-scale production, and the emphasis on diversity to ensure that there is always food for the family and community was widely discussed, especially regarding the comparative advantages of small-scale agriculture that is diverse and oriented mainly to local production. Also evident was everyone's desire to persevere despite what it means to resist the temptation to give in to the monoculture of sugarcane.

Many mentioned the frequent conversations with neighbors and relatives with nearby plots, asking them to stop renting their land for sugarcane—which impoverishes and hardens the soil—and return to diversified food production to supply nearby and other communities. They see older adults as a great resource for the community, not only because of their knowledge and wisdom but because they can still participate in the productive process. An example is the Agua Azul community, which has started a family garden project led by older adults, making the patios that surround the homes productive. At this moment, they have around 20 gardens.

In Norte del Cauca, not all plots are small; There are also larger agricultural operations. Regenerative agriculture, in any case, is not just for small plots; its principles can be applied to larger areas. For example, there is a family in Perico Negro that combines agriculture with livestock. They have learned to use everything the farm produces to achieve greater productivity. For example, they have begun to improve their plantain crops using animal manure and have built a deep well to supply water, which is also a limitation on many farms. This community project made it easier for them to irrigate their crops and allowed them to add fattening pigs and laying hens to the plot. This parcel is on its way to becoming completely diverse and profitable economically, socially, and environmentally. From this promising beginning, their interest is to improve each of the components of the farm and further increase diversity, rationally taking advantage of each space on the farm with environmental awareness. This family is convinced of the benefits of diversity and is becoming an example for others to follow.

During the visits, we were also overwhelmed by the trust people placed in FUNDAEC. In one of the first meetings, many expressed a very promising and simple sentiment that commits us greatly: FUNDAEC staff and graduates are good people who serve the community. The people's trust in these communities is the product of a longstanding relationship during which they have seen the work that has been done. FUNDAEC stands apart from those who come just to bring things but do not follow up on what happens afterward. They say the distribution of resources is important but what they appreciate the most are the training processes that produce more significant changes over time. FUNDAEC works with the community to produce changes both within people and in communities. This issue of trust in the institution also makes people interested and encourages them to respond promptly to what is being proposed.

Ever Rivera

Building off of Cristina's comments, I would like to say that we have been very dedicated to meeting regularly and maintaining a permanent dialogue with the farmers in the region. The farmers we have been meeting with feel close to FUNDAEC. Through our dialogues, you could tell they wanted to connect and be part of what we were doing to advance food production and self-sufficiency and promote regenerative agriculture. Our first conversation with the farmers was in Perico Negro. Four participants invited us to visit their different plots; later, other neighbors invited us.

A little girl was there with them, and she told us that her family also had a farm. She kept saying, "Go to mine, go to mine." So, we visited her farm, too. When we arrived, we found the fruit trees planted three to four meters apart. They said they were not getting enough sun for growth. We started talking about planting distances, and the farmers agreed that it was probably better to have six or seven meters between the trees for the sun to reach them. We stayed, talking and sharing some recommendations. Then they expressed their gratitude, saying they appreciated that we hadn't come just out of curiosity but had provided practical suggestions that truly helped them. From there, during other visits and meetings at the FUNDAEC demonstration farm, we continued sharing additional insights that increased their interest.

Then, we told them that we were going to restart and redevelop the experimental farm in Perico Negro, which had been dormant for the past decade, and inaugurate it as the Integral Farm for Regenerative Agriculture. This prospect caught their attention. We had a notebook, and they asked us to put down their names and telephone numbers to invite them to a meeting at the Integral Farm for Regenerative Agriculture to further expand this conversation and dialogue.

We have made progress in these meetings and developed an action plan with them so that work can begin on each of their farms following FUNDAEC's Integral Farm model. It is a joint learning process because elements are incorporated into the experimental farm, each is discussed at length, and certain skills are learned. For example, after talking about organic fertilizers, we carry out fertilizer preparation practices so they can replicate it on their farms to improve soil fertility. The transition on the experimental farm occurs simultaneously on the participants' farms.

These visits and gatherings confirm what the Ingenieros have said about the desire among the people in the region to reconnect with FUNDAEC. We have wanted to remodel the experimental farm in Perico Negro for some time, and we envisioned it as a place for learning more about regenerative agriculture and how to transition from conventional to the traditional forms of agriculture used by the peasants before the monocultures. However, the experimental farm, like their farms, is also in transition; it is not yet a model regenerative farm. Farmers are beginning the transition.

So, now we have the experimental farm, and they have their farms. Together, we will gradually learn the steps needed to make small transitions on these farms. This transition is a long-term process, as the soil needs regeneration, and we must make an effort to achieve it. Currently, there is little discussion about diversity on farms, so the experimental farm needs to become more diverse. That is the effort FUNDAEC is making: to demonstrate the transition at the experimental farm in Perico Negro. We can also learn from the farmers in this group about how they manage their plots and what can be improved. As the experimental farm transitions, the farmers will also be affected. But this will be a continuous dialogue. They will bring their learning from their farms to the experimental farm. This collaborative work is already underway.

We have also been meeting with and supporting several organizations. As a group, we decided to create a mural similar to the one we did at the school. The idea was to use art to promote awareness of regenerative agriculture. The following story illustrates our efforts and the community's receptivity: I went to speak with a man who owned a house with a large, highly visible wall. I knew his neighbor, a woman I had been acquainted with during my college days. I asked him for permission to use the wall, and he readily agreed, allowing us to create the mural there. Additionally, he suggested that underneath the mural, we could create a garden with flowers and aromatic herbs.

I told them we would not just come and paint; we should meet with all the neighbors there. Everything we do is like this: inviting people into the process—helping bring people together to understand what is happening rather than allowing for a great deal of gossip and miscommunication. So, we invited ten neighbors to have a conversation. We said, "Let's look at that garden; if you work together to cultivate it, it will be very nice. You can all participate as you also have patios at your houses, but it might be good to receive some training." They agreed to participate, and they want to have a garden, too. All the people participating are energizing the work. New people are coming to ask if they can join the group and participate in this project with the home gardens. The fact that this started with a mural and now ten families want to start a community plot and garden has surprised me.

I believe we are seeing a confirmation of FUNDAEC's approach to cycles of action-reflection, study, and consultation. The Growing Hope project is not small at all. But, in FUNDAEC, we start modestly, always starting with something small and organic and using a particular systematic approach: come, reflect with someone, study something, come back, consult and from there, start building something. I believe each component in this project works using this approach, consciously or unconsciously. That is what we have learned: this culture of being able to work that way. You have your consultation, you have your meetings, you study, and you don't go outside the basic framework. Gustavo has taught us that each time you do something, you have to return and reflect on it. I believe that one thing that distinguishes FUNDAEC is that it always generates knowledge through action-reflection. The knowledge acquired comes from experience: the knowledge in the PSA texts comes from experience, the knowledge that other people bring comes from their experiences, and the current experiences also contribute to future learning.

We now host home garden workshops and invite farmers to the Integral Farm for Regenerative Agriculture. We are also studying and discovering new things. We bring things people have done and whose reflections produce other learnings. I believe that the systematization team—documenting our progress—will greatly help us with this process. I feel that Growing Hope's human resources also have to be raised within that same path as they participate in the project, which always starts in organic and small ways. Each element of a project like Growing Hope has to develop its human resources to sustain it. In the early stages of this project, the human resources were us; we had to do it ourselves. But I feel we are moving into another phase and are already beginning to see people from the communities alongside us. More and more people are engaged. However, the groups in the communities have to form little by little through study and the knowledge they generate through experience. They will become more aware of everything we are doing, and we also will understand more about what we are doing. Advancing this project doesn't mean that we understand development. I learn something new every day. We are also always learning.

I believe that the issues of food production, sovereignty, and regenerative agriculture have become more evident among people. Providing food due to the pandemic crisis and its relationship to the care and preservation of the environment is a sensitive topic. When you start talking to people about food, you notice they are worried about not having food. So, being concerned about diversity and local food and promoting health resonates with them. We are harvesting a lot of experience from all of FUNDAEC's efforts over the past 50 years. FUNDAEC is in an incredible position in Norte del Cauca. When these organizations talk about FUNDAEC, they speak about it with a lot of respect. That, for me, is key. There is a lot of credibility and trust in how they perceive our work, for it is decisive. They speak very well of FUNDAEC. One could say the stars have aligned.

Haleh

I want to make mention of the agricultural capacity already built in the communities participating in Growing Hope. As Gustavo said earlier, from the start of the project, there were numerous PSA (Preparation for Social Action) groups spread throughout the country, with members well-versed in agricultural practices and community engagement. When the conversation turned to initiating practical projects for these groups, it became evident that they had the necessary skills and were keen to put their knowledge and experience into action. Their enthusiasm for engaging in projects that offered both personal benefits and the potential to uplift their communities was undeniable. This eagerness represented a golden opportunity for us to actively encourage development initiatives aimed at enhancing both the material and spiritual well-being of the communities where our students lived.

We have also explored the reasons behind the overwhelmingly positive response to our project in our team's weekly consultation and study meetings. While I can't recall all the details from our recent discussion, one notable factor is the long-standing presence of FUNDAEC in the Norte del Cauca region for the past 50 years and the crucial element of trust that Cristina and Ever have mentioned. Unlike many organizations that come and go, FUNDAEC has remained committed to providing opportunities and education to the local community, increasing people's trust that their participation will be meaningful. Another significant aspect is the impact FUNDAEC has had on education in the region, which is evident in the number of university-educated individuals and teachers who have benefited from our programs. Many people in the region have a connection to FUNDAEC through their participation in the SAT program or previous collaboration with our organization, including farmers who worked with us many years ago. As Ever and Cristina describe, the communities have welcomed FUNDAEC's presence.

During a recent meeting, a woman shared her experience as a former student at the experimental farm in Perico Negro. She highlighted how her connection with FUNDAEC, specifically through a PSA Group led by Ever, shaped her understanding of agriculture. This encounter served as a testament to the lasting impact FUNDAEC has had on individuals' lives over the years. Moreover, the current historical moment is crucial in garnering support for our initiatives. People recognize the urgent need for alternative approaches to development, especially considering the detrimental effects of certain agricultural practices and development models. While some of the concerns raised today echo sentiments from 40 or 50 years ago, there is a heightened awareness of the consequences of these approaches, leading to a renewed appreciation for FUNDAEC's sustainable and community-centric perspective. These are just a few reasons we discussed, and I'm sure more will continue to emerge as we delve deeper into our community's perceptions and experiences.

Launching a tree-planting or home gardening initiative might seem standard in environmental projects, yet many such efforts fail to incorporate crucial elements that demand quality participation. These elements range from selecting appropriate tree species and gardening sites to formulating a maintenance strategy and integrating these endeavors into the broader context of community development. These vital factors have played a key role in the success of our project.

In communities hosting PSA (Preparation for Social Action) groups, members of these groups gathered to deliberate on the types of trees to plant or crops to cultivate, considering their benefits and how they fit into the community's larger vision. In the case of tree planting, this process involved the creation of a community map to identify existing tree species and pinpoint gaps in the local biodiversity. The aim was to cultivate a varied landscape that included fruit trees and species that attract birds, enhancing ecological diversity. The home and community gardening projects also allowed PSA participants to engage with local farmers, fostering an exchange of knowledge and collaborative learning. Participants honed their research abilities and deepened their understanding of the region through this action, research, and reflection cycle. They acquired essential skills and knowledge for the sustained care of the trees, ensuring their growth and

From garden to table, Ruhi Arbab School, Puerto Tejada, Cauca, 2024

Students of the Ruhi Arbab School learning together about
establishing a vegetable garden, 2024

contribution to the community for years to come. This project's true
success lies not in the physical act of planting trees or gardens but in the
unity and cooperative spirit fostered among PSA groups and the
thoughtful attention to the communities' ecological and social fabric.
Sometimes, it is not just the qualities of the group (warp) that strengthen
the projects. Rather, the action-reflection, consultation, and study cycle

"By sowing seeds we reap life" mural created at the entrance of the Ruhi Arbab School by students, teachers, and administrators together with FUNDAEC and the Committee for the Defense of the AfroNortecaucano Territory

(weft) forged through the project strengthens the groups by pulling them together around a common cause.

I want to conclude my comments by highlighting another aspect that aligns with the theme of growing hope and the fertile ground today versus the 1970s when FUNDAEC was born. The response of the Bahá'í school in Puerto Tejada engaged in the Growing Hope project, has been remarkably encouraging and surprising. In just a few months, they have successfully established a vegetable garden with the active participation of grades six and seven, which has already begun to yield produce. Additionally, they have initiated a small research project to understand the families' food provisioning and consumption habits, conducting individual interviews and focus groups. These focus groups study content that incorporates themes related to nutrition. The school administration has also taken a significant step by eliminating sodas from the small kiosk that sells snacks to the students, opting to provide only natural fruit juices. Presently, the school prepares the juices from fruits purchased from local farmers. However, as the trees will yield fruit soon, they can utilize fruits from those planted on-site. This further underscores their commitment to promoting healthier dietary practices among the students.

Another intriguing aspect is the enthusiastic response from the teachers—many of whom have graduated from FUNDAEC's formal education programs or participated in other courses FUNDAEC has offered in the region. They possess substantial knowledge about the program's content and have wholeheartedly embraced the Growing Hope initiative. Yet, beyond the teachers' enthusiasm, what is even more surprising is the active engagement of parents. Initially skeptical about the extent of their involvement, I was taken aback when Ever informed me about the numerous projects planned with the families, from home gardening to neighborhood initiatives to school-based projects. Despite busy schedules and potential disinterest, these parents have genuinely taken the project to heart. Their enthusiasm can be attributed to various factors, including their unique circumstances and the region's distinct characteristics. The region offers a compelling environment, and the families genuinely want to take advantage of the available resources. Understanding the dynamics of this special region is certainly worth further analysis.

Bradley

Building upon what Ever, Cristina, and Haleh have shared, I believe a few additional things that have emerged from the recent cycles of action-reflection, consultation, and study is that the receptivity also comes from a certain collective awareness and dissatisfaction with the broken promises and results of past ideas, schemes, approaches, and strategies. Many people are losing faith in the designs used over the past decades and feel we, as a society, are headed in the wrong direction. The pandemic brought into relief the uncertainty in our lives. The pandemic and the shutdowns all disclosed what is constantly under the surface. It brought all the veils down, revealed an ever-underlying crisis, and revealed that things could fall apart at any moment. People were reflecting on the systems we have in place and how effective they are for fostering society's well-being. So, I think that when the pandemic happened, the institutional breakdowns confirmed what people already had felt for many years: maybe we are moving in the wrong direction.

On the other hand, FUNDAEC and the PSA groups operate at the grassroots level across Colombia and elsewhere. FUNDAEC, as an institution, has never deviated from its intention for the past 50 years, continuing its works toward the same mission and maintaining unparalleled integrity in what it does. So, when the time of uncertainty came, they were trusted by the communities. That is not to say that FUNDAEC has the answers to resolve all the problems the communities were facing. But I do believe it is the integrity of this approach that also attracts people; it's attractive. There was a renewed recognition, a rebirth, or reinvigoration of the spirit of the organization in the minds of its champions and the communities participating in its initiatives.

Working with the team on the Growing Hope project in Norte del Cauca has astonished me. Nothing escapes systematic observation by all in the team. Everyone simultaneously participates in the action-reflection, consultation, and study cycles individually and as a group. All projects and components of projects are working along timelines. Action-reflection is happening constantly, and everyone in FUNDAEC is doing research. I don't mean research in a sterile way—but in an animated and everyday concept implying inquiry, study, action and observation, reflection, thinking about implications, asking questions, and being mindful of how the projects unfold. In any other circumstance, in a project of this nature, you would see organizations do some research at the beginning and some at the end. Then, you would use these pre-/ post-assessments to draw a line between them and determine what they learned. This is how development projects all around the world evaluate their work. In FUNDAEC, however, everything learned is immediately communicated and folded back into the learning process to improve outcomes.

From my standpoint, FUNDAEC operates like an organism composed of individuals, groups, and communities highly attuned to observing, assessing, evaluating, consulting, etc. An institutional tapestry of tutors and regional and local coordinators guides FUNDAEC; people who have the training, have gone through the process and understand, have a common language for making their observations and decisions, and are committed to mutual aid and cooperation. And then you have the same capacity at the national level. Information is being shared and communicated across these different regions involved in the projects so that action and learning are being researched and knowledge generated and applied across vastly different geographies. So you don't need an individual extension agent or technical assistant running things; you have an entire living tapestry— an organic architecture of people who can communicate with one another and share and support one another to advance these projects that are regenerating agriculture from the ground up.

In West Virginia, we are only beginning to learn to approach development in this way, seeking to establish the kind of groups and learning processes presently in Norte del Cauca. Yet, we are still learning the nuances of the approach and developing the capacity to work with commitment, dedication, and quality with young people in our region. The Growing Hope project is an incredible example of its ability to build upon capacities established over generations and inspire new action today. Indeed, it renews my motivation to continue building capacity here in my home region of Appalachia.

Gustavo

We have tried to show how the Growing Hope project has advanced through action-reflection, consultation, and study—distinctive characteristics of FUNDAEC's approach in accompanying rural

Exchanging tree species, Integral Farm for Regenerative Agriculture, 2023

Visit of regional farmers to FUNDAEC's Integral Farm, 2023

Visit to the Integral Farm, farmers learning about organic fertilizers, 2023

communities in their development process. This particular approach emphasizes the dialogue of knowledges, building trust between participants, mutual agreements and commitments, generating knowledge, and developing individual and collective capabilities. As we have experienced at different times and in other projects narrated in this history, the implementation of the projects always advances in parallel with the training of Promoters of Community Well-being through the PSA program. This training enables the promoters to internalize the learning, ensuring that the transformations in the community endure beyond the project's conclusion.

The Growing Hope project illustrates our participatory approach and demonstrates how FUNDAEC has consistently maintained its perspective on the role of agriculture in the comprehensive development of a region since 1974. Its efforts have aimed to promote agriculture that focuses on food security while generously rewarding the farmer. The value and importance of the farmer—as the first link in the production chain and the main producer of food—cannot be underestimated. We are convinced that farmers are the foundation on which the food security of any society is built. Their hard and dedicated work ensures that food reaches our tables, providing not only nutrition but also economic and social stability.

Likewise, farmers play a crucial role in environmental sustainability by implementing responsible agricultural practices that protect and regenerate the land. As custodians of the earth, their knowledge and skills are essential to maintaining biodiversity and ecosystem health. Valuing the farmer and elevating the dignity of agricultural work implies investing in the training, technology, and resources necessary to confront modern challenges, such as climate change and market fluctuations. For

FUNDAEC, the farmer has always been considered the foundation of society's organization.

The effects of the Growing Hope project are visible in various aspects of community life and reflect what is happening below the ground and in the natural environment. If the soil erodes and loses vitality, water will be diminished and contaminated; if forests wither and are cut down, biodiversity will be compromised. If deeply rooted practices that contribute to these imbalances are insisted upon, the community will begin to manifest the interrelated symptoms of ailments that affect its physical, emotional, and spiritual wellbeing. These symptoms include the impact on food security and its corresponding derivatives, the anguish of seeing the futility of the effort invested in agricultural work, the detachment from the land in the new generations, and the emergence of a social climate that favors inequalities, weakens the ties that unite people, and that entrenches violence.

Likewise, an isolated, alienated, and dissociated community creates soil with the characteristics of degeneration, and all of these characteristics are exacerbated by the situation of the earth itself becoming diseased. However, the farmers, neighbors, teachers, and collaborating associations we work with long to regenerate the land and the society around them. This approach shared across generations, young and old, has given new life to relationships in Norte del Cauca. We are seeing a flourishing of activities around agriculture where people are gaining new confidence and a hopeful outlook.

Through the Growing Hope project, our team has seen that regenerative agriculture requires a different way of viewing the land and surrounding landscape. It is about promoting a diverse and balanced environment that encourages the natural processes of healthy soil free of toxins and rich in organic matter and biodiversity. Studies have sufficiently demonstrated that the practices resulting from this conception of agriculture substantially improve soil productivity and the quality of products and, therefore, income—while preserving soil fertility in the long term. The healthy land, in turn, manifests the complementarity of the spiritual and the material. The survival of species requires solidarity, cooperation, and mutual aid. It is an integrated whole where each part plays a role in preserving biological diversity and life. The practice of regenerative agriculture increases understanding of the intricate web of relationships on earth, leading to the formation of equivalent relationships between people: relationships of solidarity, cooperation, and mutual support. A change in the heart occurs, giving rise to the love for the land characteristic of peasant communities worldwide. At FUNDAEC, we understand that this transformation process, already underway, will take a long time and requires tenacity, joint effort, and deep conviction. Even so, we are sure that the best catalyst for this process will be the measurable and tangible results that are already beginning to manifest in the lands and communities of Norte del Cauca.

Growing Hope is a modest project in its scale that supports four communities in Norte del Cauca in their efforts to remove themselves from what is causing these evils and work with children, youth, teachers, and parents from three schools in the region, accompanying them to take actions that are within their reach aimed at the production, transformation, and consumption of healthy foods—an essential component of what they intend to do. We hope that a model will emerge from the learnings of these years that will also allow other communities to benefit.

Now, a few words about the future. FUNDAEC, as a learning institution, will continue to stay true to its mission of accompanying rural and urban communities on their path to comprehensive development. Unlike in 1974, when it began, today, it is building on a solid foundation alongside thousands of graduates who have internalized a particular vision of development and equipped themselves with the intellectual and technical capabilities necessary to invite others to join this noble enterprise. As the network of participants—students, tutors, and institutions—expands and consolidates, the flow of information, knowledge, and enthusiasm will accelerate in all directions. The achievements and efforts of each group will make the evolving development strategy more visible.

FUNDAEC will continue to systematize learning through complementary content to its existing educational materials, ensuring that they are quickly incorporated into discourse and into local development initiatives and projects. The model being developed in the four communities of Norte del Cauca, together with the three schools in which the activities of the Growing Hope project are carried out, will occupy the attention and resources of FUNDAEC in the coming years. Within the conception of regenerative agriculture, the work will demand—based on what was previously experienced in the Norte del Cauca region—rigorously advancing the different components of the local economy. Small-scale food production for self-consumption, the generation of surpluses, product marketing systems that equitably benefit participants, and the creation and strengthening of social and economic structures in the region will be priorities. The effort to provide access to education for the entire population at various levels through the PSA program and other programs will continue to be a priority over the years.

Postscript

By Gustavo Correa

To conclude this narrative that Haleh, Bradley, and I have brought together, we decided that I would pen a few closing words about our enriching experience of collective book writing. Although these words are presented in the first person, I have endeavored to encapsulate the feelings and reflections of my two dear friends as well. Our original goal was to pinpoint some pivotal moments in the journey of FUNDAEC, bringing to memory significant events and individuals who over the past 50 years played key roles in these stories. We anticipated that this would conclude with the publication of this manuscript. However, as we explored the edges of our memories, we realized that we were engaging in something far greater than a project that came to a certain conclusion. As we uncovered various threads from our conversations, we began to see new patterns, textures, and colors emerge from the efforts woven over half a century, revealing a rich tapestry to which we hope others in future generations will continue to add further experiences and insights.

At a personal level, I have been reflecting fondly on the many individuals who contributed, and I have been pondering the intensity of moments I have lived alongside others working in this enterprise. Returning to these memories has been immensely fulfilling. It has heightened my awareness of many transformations catalyzed by FUNDAEC over the past 50 years. These individual and collective transformations were just dreams at the outset of our journey in the 1970s. Communities once defined by particular social, economic, and environmental constraints are now recognized for their residents' spirit, capacity, enthusiasm, and collective resolve to forge a future for which they had yearned. The process of writing the book also reaffirmed my belief in the central role of education in any development project—an educational process tailored to meet a community's needs, which empowers individuals and unveils their hidden potentialities. While we have done our best to reveal many stories and sought to capture the impact of these transformations, we also know that the effects of these efforts extend well beyond what has been recorded and can be recollected within the limits set by our own vision.

Yet, I still feel a sense of obligation when considering that our written work merely skims the surface of a legacy rich with deep and layered stories. There are countless individuals whose tales would enrich this document, but constraints of time and space prevented their inclusion. The Ingenieros, in particular, are highlighted in the narrative as early pioneers on this journey. However, this does not overshadow the numerous other key players, both prominent and unseen, whose determined actions over decades form an integral part of our institutional legacy. Those who came from other regions and countries, who became champions of development in their own right, the tutors and administrators who lead the cause of education for development, and the farmers and graduates whose conviction and faith continue to inspire those currently in the field—they all have played a crucial role.

On a personal note, it has been comforting to engage more closely with the long-standing and more recent contributors who are now scripting the next chapters of FUNDAEC's story. This interaction has served as a salve for the longing that often accompanies memories of past colleagues and fleeting moments. The hope and desire to continue building unity ignited in the new generations by our story is perhaps our greatest reward, a serendipitous gift. Over the years, those of us who founded FUNDAEC were clear that while people and institutions may pass, the ideas must endure. These ideas have become part of a global discourse on development, a legacy that new actors must carry forward and enrich.

It is our hope that this book will serve not only those directly engaged with FUNDAEC's programs but also many elders who have dedicated their lives to the common good and many of the younger generation now at pivotal moments in their lives as they envision their future careers. Every socially conscious individual faces the dilemma of how to devote their diverse talents to the common good. Each person must find their own answer, considering their own capabilities and the opportunities and possibilities that lay before them. Working for the common good is challenging, fraught with obstacles and persistent doubts. While many highlight the sacrifices involved in such work, from my long-standing perspective, the notion of sacrifice diminishes as the progress of others becomes the most rewarding outcome of our efforts. Were I to revisit the decision I made 50 years ago to leave a career in mathematics for rural development work, I would choose the same path again. In closing, I wish to offer the following thought, which has inspired me through these years, excerpted from the Bahá'í writings:

...the happiness and greatness, the rank and station, the pleasure and peace of an individual have never consisted in his personal wealth, but rather in his excellent character, his high resolve, the breadth of his learning, and the ability to solve difficult problems...

Bibliography

Arbab, Farzam. (1984). *Rural university: learning about education and development*. Ottawa: IDRC.

Arbab, Farzam. (1991) *La senda del aprendizaje en Latinoamérica: opción moral.* Colombia: Editorial Nur.

Arbab, Farzam. (2000) 'Promoting a discourse on science, religion, and development' in Harper, Sharon M. P. (ed.) *The lab, the temple, and the market: Reflections at the intersection of science, religion, and development.* Canada: IDRC; Europe and the United States: Kumarian Press.

Ashraf, Nava, Banerjee, Abhijit, and Nourani, Vesall. (2023) *Learning to teach by learning to learn.* [Unpublished working paper]. University of Chicago and Makerere University.

Benjamin, Walter. (1940/2020) 'Theses on the philosophy of history', in Bronner, Stephen E. and Kellner, Douglas M. (eds.) *Critical theory and society: A reader.* New York: Routledge, pp. 255-263.

Bohm, David. (1980/2003) *Wholeness and the implicate order.* New York: Routledge.

Chambers, Robert. (1983/2014) *Rural development: Putting the last first.* New York: Routledge.

Critchfield, Richard. (1983) *Villages.* New York: Anchor Books.

Horton, Myles. (1990) *We make the road by walking: Conversations on education and social change.* Philadelphia: Temple University Press.

Karlberg, Michael. and Correa, Bita. (2016) 'Development as systematic learning and capacity building', in Skinner, Amy , Smith Matt B., Brown, Eleanor and Troll, Tobias. *Education, learning and the transformation of development.* New York: Routledge, pp. 19-35.

Schumacher, E. F. (1973/2011) *Small is beautiful: A study of economics as if people mattered.* New York: Random House.

Taussig, Michael T. (1980/2010) *The devil and commodity fetishism in South America.* Chapel Hill: The University of North Carolina Press.

White, Monica M. (2018) *Freedom farmers: Agricultural resistance and the Black freedom movement.* Chapel Hill: The University of North Carolina Press.

About the Book

Weaving a Fabric of Unity describes the pioneering enterprise that became the Foundation for the Application and Teaching of Science, known as FUNDAEC. The book highlights action and learning from five decades of FUNDAEC's experience, through stories told by and about individuals engaged in shaping its work. The authors discuss some of the underlying concepts of FUNDAEC's unique methodological approach, which focuses on the integration of theory and practice and on releasing human potentialities. They take the reader on a journey through FUNDAEC's creation of one of Latin America's most innovative rural education and development programs. Additionally, they narrate ways in which FUNDAEC's focus on raising up individuals and populations dedicated to the promotion of community well-being supported its efforts to scale organically over the last few decades. This approach allowed its programs to reach hundreds of thousands of students across Colombia and to be adopted in over a dozen countries globally to support diverse populations working towards the collective realization of a dignified future.

About the Authors

Gustavo Correa began his career as a mathematics professor at the Universidad del Valle in Cali, Colombia. Gustavo was one of the founders of FUNDAEC in 1974 and served as its director from 1988 to 2005. He is the co-author of a number of educational materials produced by FUNDAEC. In 2008 he was elected to the Universal House of Justice, the international governing council of the Bahá'í Faith, which he served until 2018. Since his return to Colombia in 2018, Gustavo has continued as an advisor to FUNDAEC and other development and education organizations. Among current endeavors, he helped mobilize a network of 1,500 people across 800 initiatives to quickly respond to the food insecurity problem triggered by COVID-19 in Colombia. This project, Growing Hope, is one of the key inspirations for this book.

Gustavo holds a Master's degree in Public Administration from Harvard University's Kennedy School of Government.

Dr. Bradley Wilson is Associate Professor of Geography and Executive Director of the West Virginia University Center for Resilient Communities. For 20 years Bradley has conducted research in Nicaragua, Colombia, and West Virginia on the response of communities to regional economic crises and the central role of solidarity, mutual aid, grassroots initiatives, and social movements in forging alternative rural development pathways in those regions. In recent years he has embraced his identity as a participatory action researcher–working in teams to accompany community partners as they work for social change. With his students he has established a robust action research program focused on cooperative economics, food justice, food system development, community health, and environmental justice in West Virginia and Appalachia. For the past five years, Bradley has collaborated with FUNDAEC on projects focused on its educational programs and building the capacity of its research teams working on food sovereignty in Norte del Cauca.

Bradley holds a PhD in Geography from Rutgers University.

Dr. Haleh Arbab has over four decades of experience as a leader in education for development. Haleh worked for FUNDAEC from 1982 to 2005, including ten years as director of its Centro Universitario de Bienestar Rural (The University Center for Rural Wellbeing), a Colombian university she co-founded in 1988 that offered over 3,000 students undergraduate and graduate degree programs in education for development. From 2005 to 2018, Haleh served as director of the Institute for Studies in Global Prosperity (ISGP), where she participated in efforts to elaborate and promote a Discourse on Science, Religion, and Development in collaboration with international NGOs, government officials, and academics. At ISGP, she also worked on the design, implementation, and evaluation of graduate and undergraduate seminars focused on equipping students on six continents to contribute to constructive social change. She is currently the founding director of the Center for Research in Education for Development (CRED). Her current work focuses on fostering community-based approaches to research and education internationally.

Haleh holds a Doctor of Education from the Center for International Education at the University of Massachusetts and a Master's degree in Communications from the University of Pennsylvania.